On the Way Out

Jack McCall and Alan Clement

On the Way Out

iUniverse books may be ordered through booksellers or by contacting:

iUniverse
1663 Liberty Drive
Bloomington, IN 47403
www.iuniverse.com
1-800-Authors (1-800-288-4677)

Cover photo: Alan Hausenflock Photography

ISBN: 978-1-4759-2749-8 (sc)
ISBN: 978-1-4759-2751-1 (e)
ISBN: 978-1-4759-2750-4 (hc)

Library of Congress Control Number: 2012909323

Print information available on the last page.

iUniverse rev. date: 02/14/2018

Introduction

Two walks of life.

John R. *Jack* McCall was born to be a priest, because his father wanted it so bad.

Alan Clement was born a Catholic, because that's what his mother was.

Jack became a Jesuit, and spent thirty years studying and teaching other young Jesuits. He earned a doctorate in theology and another in clinical psychology, a rare combination. He also cultivated a rare sense of humor which marked his ability to get a point across, a skill put to good use in the thirty years following his priesthood when he became the chief psychologist for the prison system of North Carolina; then later, a favorite speaker for corporate audiences across the continent.

Alan grew up in his father's sign shop, a haven for men who engaged in various expressions of humor while lettering signs. He later ran his own creative group in marketing communications, mostly writers and designers and illustrators who engaged in the same kind of banter while producing winning campaigns for companies and colleges.

He lost that promising business in a national program for the Church and later became a corporate spokesman, speech coach, actor, free-lancer, and on occasion, taxi driver in New York City.

In their growing up years, they both experienced the same hard times, the Depression years of the 1930s. Jack's family never owned a home, always rented. In fact, the day his parents first brought him home from the hospital, the family was ejected, because the landlady, Mrs. Berkowitz, did not want a squalling child in her building. They moved five times during his school years, from one small, barely adequate apartment in Bridgeport to another.

Alan was raised in a small town outside of Buffalo, in a house like every other third house on the block. He delivered newspapers, as his three older brothers had done, and hung out in the shop, a four-door garage behind the Irving house, the first, oldest and biggest house on the block. It was around the corner from the drug store and across the street from the grammar school. When he collected the weekly stipend for his paper route, eighteen cents for six newspapers, he got to know his customers, mostly young couples with young families, and to connect the kitchen aromas with the nationalities.

Jack was very popular at school. He was elected president of the student council three years running, mostly because of his sense of humor, rather than any intellectual achievement. He hung out in the school library reading plays when he wasn't playing baseball in the school yard. On graduating, he had to make a tough decision between entering the Jesuits or entering the Army with his buddies. He chose the former. Fortunately, they all survived the World War II years.

WWII ended during the 15th week of Alan's 16-week basic training in the Infantry. He was sent over to Europe immediately to replace the boys coming back, including one of his brothers. He had not distinguished himself academically in high school, but played football and basketball, had a wonderful girlfriend for two years, got good marks in English, but had real struggles with math and science.

Looking back, it could be said that the strong influence for both came from their fathers. Jack's was a strict Catholic, a loyal bank employee, content with a steady paycheck, a no risk guy, but a good saver who lost his total investments in the stock market crash. He meanwhile insisted that Jack provide a talk after dinner almost every evening, standing on the riser in front of the false fireplace, starting with a strong opening line, then providing the important lesson learned. Facing an audience became old hat for Jack.

Rudy, Alan's father, had always worked hard, physically, to support his growing family. There were snapshots of him lettering chimneys rising high above a factory and swinging in a bos'ns chair while lettering the town's name on a water tower. He was "good with his hands," an expression popular at the time, one which was later applied to Alan, unwittingly, by his girlfriend. Rudy was a good leader in the shop, often guiding the men in their personal struggles, as well as their skills in lettering. One previously rode the rails from racetrack to racetrack across the country, another two were victims of booze. He rarely offered much advice to his sons, advocating that they learn their lessons the hard way.

Jack's father spent most evenings at night school or in the public library, striving to advance in the banking business. Rudy would retreat to the basement work bench and letter paper signs for the windows of the butcher shop and other merchants. During the holidays when the outdoor sign business slowed down because of the snow and ice, he would build a Christmas surprise in the basement, one year a ping pong table, another year a bowling alley using Canadian duckpins and leaded croquet balls. In the back yard, he built a giant slide and a swing that stood 15 feet off the ground.

Jack often said that his parents were not very affectionate, toward him or one another. Alan's were affectionate, but not so much toward one another in later life. Once the empty nest took place, they picked at each other like so many parents do.

That's a background in brief. The themes that reveal themselves in the conversations of these two men in their upper 80s often hinge on faith and religion, maybe the difference in faith and religion. The fun they had in being open and honest in talking about free will and conjecturing about the life hereafter and simply talking about issues that men rarely talk about translates into fun for the reader as well.

People often ask how these two men met. It was in a retirement home. Jack and Mary were staying there, for a short period as it turned out, and Alan was creating portrait sculptures in the activity room every Friday afternoon.

Mary brought Jack with her one day, he joined Alan in delighting the ladies, and a few men, with their stories, and the rest is history.

Following are a years' worth of weekly conversations, almost all of which were transcribed directly from taped recordings; the first two or three were edited from notes. There was no attempt to organize the conversations in advance; the intent was to let them happen. The two men had a pretty good idea that they would be talking about life wrapped around free will, their purpose in life, the meaning of life, and. because of their ages, the life hereafter. During that year, Jack's beloved wife, Mary, was suffering the effects of Parkinson's. She died in December, 2009. Jack died a few months later, on the eve of his 90th birthday, from the effects of a broken neck suffered in an auto accident.

Alan had promised to gather the conversations, and this is the result. The hope is that you will picture these two characters and hear them talking as you read their words.

Contents

Fateful Year 1968

J: I was thinking how the turning points in each of our lives occurred during the same years.

A: Yes. The years following Vatican II.

J: I left the Jesuits, which was a heart-wrenching experience for me.

A: And I lost my business, family, and ultimately, my self-worth.

J: It was in 1968 that I began to realize that things were changing in my heart and my head. Up until then, I was still rigid in my thinking.

A: That was the same year I lost it all, in a program for the church. My little company had a contract to launch the New Catholic Encyclopedia to the laity, across the country. Sixteen-volume work, nothing like it since 1906. Our advance program was keyed to Christmas delivery, 1968.

J: Really? That was the most difficult Christmas of my life. I had met my close friend, another priest I had studied with early on, and we walked the beach. We were down at Hatteras. It was cold, but we bundled up and walked for miles, talking about our doubts, our questions, honest and open, but heart-breaking at the same time.

A: I can imagine.

J: We were questioning everything, but it was good. It didn't shake our faith. I say that, but we both became a lot more open in our approach to religion as such. I'd always taught by opening up the floor to questions, and I was always confident that I could lead them back to the answers.

A: Is that when you left the order?

J: No, not right away. Pope John 23rd, who opened the door to let some fresh air in, he died in 1963, you remember, and then John Paul, who followed, was busy *closing* the door on any new idea or thought that would challenge the old way of doing things.

A: He put a real crimp in our program, as well. But that's another story.

J: I want to hear it.

A: Yours first. Mine goes on forever.

J: Mine, too. Most of us carried on, but the light had gone out. We had rejoiced with Vatican Two, it had given us new hope, that we would be relevant, open and honest in keeping with the problems and challenges of the times. Television alone had accelerated the attitudes, the upheaval in the thinking of our young people, hippies and free love, the war in Korea, which no one understood, the rush to go out and buy products advertised on TV. It was a time of change, and there we were, going backwards.

A: I remember. That was the sorriest Christmas I ever had, as well. We had positioned the encyclopedia as a secular work, even had Bishops from the other denominations invited to the dinner events we arranged in each major diocese throughout the country. All keyed to Christmas delivery. Each worthy family received a four-color brochure on Thanksgiving describing the 16 volumes they would be receiving as a Christmas present one month later, from a thoughtful donor. You know, a wealthy lay leader.

J: So what happened?

A: The publisher, McGraw-Hill, informed us the day after Thanksgiving that they would not be able to make delivery, that they were behind schedule. All the time they had been sending galleys indicating that they were right on schedule.

J: What did you do?

A: Well, first we had to call the lay leaders and ask if they wanted us to inform the families or if they wanted to do it, either way a big embarrassment to the very people we were depending on to advance the program.

J: Sounds like you had a case against the publisher.

A: Interesting you should ask. My neighbor and close friend was the top attorney in the legal firm whose major client was the Marine Bank, the bank that provided the loan to me, almost two hundred thousand dollars. He took it on, but then his firm declined, stating that they couldn't afford to fight McGraw-Hill's battery of sixty eight lawyers who would stretch out the case for seven or eight years, and there wouldn't be enough money in it to even support the fight. I heard the same reasoning from two other legal firms.

J: Wow, you were left holding the bag?

A: Yes. The whole program depended on the sales in the advance program. We couldn't deliver, so there were no sales. To say nothing of the ill will emanating from our prime market, the lay leaders. They were embarrassed and unhappy.

J: What did you do?

A: Once over the shock, and anger, and depths of despair, I realized I had to raise some money to carry us until we had some product to sell. The bank wasn't interested in my problem, so I went to see several of the key Bishops who had been enthusiastic supporters of the program. But they begged off as far as advancing any money. At the same time, I was trying to set up an appointment with Bishop O'Boyle in Washington, the sponsor of the program in the first place. His Secretary, Father O'Connell, kept putting me off, until, finally, I told him I would be on the first flight in the morning, and I would sit with him in his office until he could fit me in for a few minutes with His Eminence. Which is exactly what happened. He made me sit there all day, until 4:20 in the afternoon, at which time he said, "All right, you can go in now, but you'll have just five minutes with him, because His Eminence leaves sharply at 4:30. Tight schedule, "He likes to have dinner watching the six o'clock news."

J: I'm starting to feel the tension.

A: Get the picture. Here I am entering this huge, magnificent, palatial office, with Oriental rugs and expensive wall hangings, bronze and marble statues and a mahogany desk that had to be 20' wide rising majestically toward Heaven, of course. It sat on an elevated platform. The visitor sat looking up at His Eminence. This desperate young man, who had worked five years in developing a golden program and traveling the country to make it happen – needed even less than five minutes to describe what happened and ask for an advance. The Bishop lifted his excess weight from the chair, motioned for the visitor to follow along, put a sympathetic hand on his back, ushered him to the door, and said, "God bless you, young man, for the work you're doing, but we have no money for this sort of thing. I'm already asking each of the pastors in the Diocese to come up with $10,000 to come to Rome and see me get my red cap."

J: He said that?

A: Verbatim. Those words, and the way he said them, have been ingrained in my memory ever since.

(long silence)

J: I'm sorry you had to re-live that.

A: I'm okay now. But I've never really recovered.

J: You're still living with the loss? No one would ever know it.

A: In the last 20 years, I've been reunited with the Lord. But I wasn't, back then. I was convinced that the Lord had rejected me, that he was punishing me for past sins. I not only lost my business, which was made up of some wonderfully creative people, the house and cars along with it, but I lost my family. I was in a deep funk, today we'd call it depression, and so difficult to live with that my wife took the kids and went South to be near her sister's family. Two of the people in my group worked part-time with me for several months to close some sales and repay most of the loan. At that point, the president of the bank suggested that I go into bankruptcy, that the bank would forget the rest. He remembered that, years before, I had been into my presentation only eight minutes when he interrupted and asked, "How much do you need?" John Galvin was his name. A really fine, decent, caring man. Not what you'd picture today as a bank president.

J: You said that you felt that the Lord had rejected you.

A: Yes, that I wasn't worthy.

J: You expected some help from Heaven?

A: Yes. I admit that. The Encyclopedia would have helped a lot of families. The editor, Father John Whalen, also a Jesuit like you, was determined to make it a family publication, and there was a lot in the volumes directed to young people, not just a stuffy repeat of the 1906 version that would sit idle on library shelves.

J: And you would have made some money.

A: Oh, absolutely. Not a killing, but we had projected that in the ensuing five years, we would have paid back the loan and have almost a hundred thousand in the bank. That was big money then.

J: Instead, you were wiped out and you lost your family.

A: I was dead broke. Deep in debt. Add to that the fact that I was always a confused Catholic. A lot of guilt and punishment and going to hell if you think a bad thought. I had a wonderful girlfriend in high school, and I felt her up as often as I could, but on the way home I would ask the Lord for forgiveness.

J: That's as accurate a description of a confused Catholic that I've ever heard.

A: You've heard a lot of confessions. You know what I mean.

J: I've been on the other side of the Confessional as well.

A: But yes, I was left feeling that I wasn't worthy enough to expect any help from God even if whatever I might be involved in would do a lot of good. It was kind of a kick in the groin to remind me that we're not doing God's work down here. God will do his work just fine without our help. We're expected to do good work because it's good.

J: Is that the way you feel now?

A: Yes, for the most part. I like to feel that the Lord is with me when I'm dealing with other people and their problems, but even there I recognize that my value as a good listener is directly related to the mistakes I've made in life, the failures, big and small, not that I'm a purveyor of good example.

J: You mentioned before that the last twenty years have been rewarding, but not the years in between. What were you doing right after the loss, from that fateful year for both of us, 1968, until 1988?

A: Downhill, man. All the time I was in New York City. A former client, a great guy named John Slaven, who was then the Director of Advertising for Volkswagen, had set up an interview for me, and I became Creative Director of a large promotion firm. I was there three weeks when the owner died of a heart attack and the firm was sold out from under us. Back on the street. I hadn't recovered from the loss of my business, and here I am in the big city where nobody knows me. I was suddenly a free-lancer, scratching for assignments, making the rounds of advertising agencies and marketing and promotion firms.

J: I'll bet that's when you started driving taxis at night.

A: I'll bet you're right. Then, on a whim, I auditioned for a job as a spokesman for major companies and was hired. That saved my life. Later I started coaching executives in speaking, and I made a living, but I never really recovered. I was still rejecting the Lord, because I felt he had rejected me. I resented the Lord. I felt that every major disappointment thereafter was an affirmation of his disdain for me, and so, of course, I was always in a downward spiral. But to most people, on the surface I was a smiling, creative, almost carefree individual. Only those close to me recognized the reality and often suffered the hurt involved.

J: You're talking about relationships?

A: Yes. You remember that I had remarried on the rebound. I knew it was a mistake after a few months, but when we learned that we were about to become parents, we stayed together. For three and a half years. Then we split and shared a wonderful daughter, back and forth every Wednesday, for many years. That little girl is now in her thirty's, still a bright light in my life, along with my older daughter who never gave up on me.

J: That doesn't sound like bad relationships.

A: No, not bad at all, but there is hurt in every relationship, you know that, with your experience as a psychologist. I had another long relationship with another wonderful woman who was like a stepmother to my daughter. We agreed not to commit, but of course, if you live together you're committing, just without official sanction. There was hurt there, too, much of it reflecting my stubborn refusal to open the door to our Lord.

J: It's difficult for others to understand what is going on in another's life. We all have a story, probably several stories.

A: Yes. There are similarities, I think, in the feelings involved. A different kind of loss can evoke the same kind of feeling for two different people.

J: Good example might be the loss of a close friend for one, loss of a great job for another. Hearing your story aroused a lot of feelings about mine.

A: It's your turn.

J: I had to think, when you were talking, that my loss was also relational. I was married to the Jesuit order. Really. I was in love with the Jesuit life. I had wanted to be a priest from the time I was young, and I was reaping the rewards of that life. I loved what I was doing. How many of us can say that?

A: Very few.

J: So giving it up was the farthest thing from my mind. I was sold. It's hard to imagine, now, but back in the sixties my belief system was set in stone: that the Catholic Church would never change, the Catholic schools would never close; that the death penalty was just and was a deterrent; I acknowledged that minorities were treated as second-class citizens, yes, but that they could rise up and make a good life for themselves, that it was quite possible for them to get a good education; that women had to work a little harder, but there were no real obstacles to their advancement, and they didn't really have to work, because their husbands would support them, and that there was no need for them to seek the freedom of choosing legal abortions.

A: That was all typical thinking of the times.

J: I was a conservative Catholic. But fortunately, I began to question a lot of things. Like the Vietnam War, the brutal treatment Blacks received when marching peacefully, our use of nuclear weapons, the growing financial gap between the very wealthy and the very poor, and on a personal basis, I began to experience the contrast between the fresh thinking of Vatican Two and what I had been taught in moral theology, scripture study and Church Law.

A: Fresh air.

J: The assassinations brought it all home. First, JFK in 1963, then both Bobby Kennedy and Martin Luther King in that fateful year, 1968. There was a major shift taking place in the Catholic Church, and I had made a large turn to the left. Now I wanted to experience a personal relationship with God, to discern his will for me, and how to see God in everyone and everything, and see everything in God, and to work on my self-deception.

A: If only we could all see God in everyone else.

J: Let me digress a minute. You were talking about the same feelings of failure and disappointment, dating back to the loss, remaining with you through all the years that followed, and still with you today. You know, that would be difficult for most people to understand. Just get over it! But I was reminded of an experience of my own that brought it home. I received a call one day, oh, this goes way back, probably nineteen sixty, from an older woman who started by saying she wasn't Catholic and had never spoken to a priest. She was grieving the loss of her thirty six year old daughter who had just committed suicide. I didn't interrupt, but I wondered what it had to do with me. She had read in her daughter's will that she had set aside money to fly me to Alabama to officiate at her funeral. Then it dawned on me. I had given a retreat in Florida, probably four or five years earlier, and her daughter had attended. She came up after one of the sessions, and we talked for about fifteen minutes, and met twice more over that weekend. She was a college professor, and appeared to others to be well adjusted, but she was also a lesbian, and she was suffering a continuous series of crushing disappointments. She had converted to Catholicism, and her intense guilt was killing her. She felt that she was constantly displeasing God because of her disoriented life. Not unlike your experience. I tried to help her realize that she was a good person and deeply loved by God, an exceptional and compassionate teacher. She simply needed to be accepted by a faith community, and she wasn't. Even today, the Church hasn't been able to accept homosexuals and lesbians. That's wrong. Jesus was always inclusive, not exclusive.

A: That was a meaningful, powerful event in your life.

J: It was an awakening. A turning point.

A: A wake-up call from the Lord.

J: Exactly. Exactly. I had never before felt such a distinct, personal message. From that point on, I was able to regard the Lord as a loving and forgiving spirit rather than a judge ready to pounce on a person's failings.

A: It's always amazing to me to learn, over and over again, how suffering in one life can lead to good in others.

Being There

J: You never talk about your Stephen Ministry experiences.

A: Well, we're trained not to, because of the confidentiality thing. No one knows who we're meeting with, unless, of course, the care-receiver tells someone, which sometimes happens.

J: But you are sworn to secrecy?

A: Yes. It's sometimes difficult for my wife and me not to exchange some thoughts, but we never acknowledge anything or even attempt to guess who each of us is meeting with. Our job is to help them get their lives in order while they're going through a real trial.

J: I can see where that would be important to them. They can unload knowing it will go no farther.

A. Right. The only exceptions are when the family of a care receiver who died, for example, gives us permission to talk about the experience. They realize how helpful that might be to someone else going through a similar trial.

J: Give me an example.

A: Well, I was assigned to a man with ALS during the last year of his life. I was fortunate to get him to open up to his family during that time. He had never been able to express his real feelings toward them, and it made a big difference in their lives.

J: I'll bet.

A: He and I had some wonderful exchanges, not unlike you and me, but he had never talked openly about some of the things you and I talk about. Relationships, religion, temptations, failures, you know, all that good stuff.

J: Wonderful.

A: After the first couple of months, I started bringing my sculpture stand, and I sculpted a bust of him while we were talking. His wife keeps it on the mantle.

J: You're still in touch with the family?

A: Yes. His son treats me like a grandfather. That often happens. I've made a lot of close friends through Stephen Ministry.

J: Tell me more.

A: Well, I was assigned to a young man, he was about 35 at the time, who had just come home from the hospital after having a brain tumor removed. I learned later that he had waited almost eight months, searching for a surgeon who would attempt the operation, because the tumor was so big.

J: Wow.

A: The first time I went to see him, I rang the doorbell three times, waiting what seemed like forever in between, meanwhile taking in kind of a run-down apartment complex on a cold, rainy, miserable day. I was about to give up when the door opened, and there stood this tall, good looking young man, but already pale and gaunt and almost ghost-like, lifeless.

J: I'm getting the picture.

A: I introduced myself, as the Stephen minister assigned to him. He kind of half-nodded and shuffled into the living room. Sat on a couch, his eyes on the floor, between his slippers. I explained how the program works, that I would be there to be the good listener once a week. No response, his eyes still on the floor. A good five minutes went by, then ten. A black cat that looked more like a brown and tan monkey, jumped up on the back of the couch and nestled in behind him, glaring at me, literally.

J: Not exactly a warm welcome.

A: I made a couple more attempts, with a ten and twenty minute wait in between. He hadn't said a word, finally he got up and shuffled toward the door. I followed, opened the door, turned to him and asked, expecting the worst, if he wanted me to come back the next week. He looked at me for the first time and nodded his head vigorously.

J: What a start.

A: It wasn't much better the next week. His eyes came off the floor a few times.

J: Whew.

A: The third week when he shuffled me into the living room, he stopped short, bent over awkwardly and shouted out to no one, half-crying, "I'm so sick and tired of wearing this damned hairpiece!" Out of the blue, just like that. It hadn't even occurred to me that he was wearing one. I tried not to show my shock and said, "Well, take it off."

J: Did he?

A: No, no. But now he was looking at me. Glaring at me. In a rage, he shouts in my face, "Sure," he says, gesturing wildly a big U above his head, "I've got one ugly scar up here, don't you understand?!"

J: Whooee.

A: After a good long minute staring at me, he seemed to settle down, and I said, "I've seen ugly scars before. I was married to a woman who had fifteen of them, one for every summer of her school years."

J: You were?

A: Yes. That slowed him down. After a long pause, he pointed up to his hairpiece and said, quietly "Really?" I said, "Really." With that, he got to his feet, yanked the hairpiece off his head and threw it in the corner. He looked at me, smiling and laughing, then came over and hugged me.

J: My God, what a story.

A: From that moment on, I couldn't stop him from talking. He told me all about waiting months for someone willing to operate and the fact that the surgeon who did operate now gives him only five months to live and how he is now trying to come to grips with that. He wanted to be heroic, you know, or at least noble, but the reality of no more wild life was setting in.

J: Wild life?

A: He had an interesting, if not productive, history of adoring ladies, booze, pot and good times. During his high school years, he was a lifeguard at his father's country club, and he kept that job, part-time of course, for many years thereafter.

J: The hunting ground.

A: No hunting required. They were there for the picking. He was accepted at a college known for its conservative Presbyterian flavor, a fact he somehow missed, and he became the campus protestor against Vietnam and almost everything else. They asked him to leave after his second year. A series of fill-in jobs followed, for several years. A series of girlfriends followed as well, punctuated with booze and pot and parties. He woke up to the fact at age 32 that he had been having fun while his peers were advancing in their careers.

J: Finally!

A: That's when he took himself back to college. There again, he was the object of a lot of female attention. Tending bar at night, no stranger to booze and pot, but also hitting the books. He was in the stands at a football game when he first passed out. Nobody thought too much of it, because of his lifestyle, but when it happened twice more that week in class, he went to see the campus doctor and ultimately found out about the tumor.

J: Talk about a shock.

A: Fast forward to the hairpiece. We agreed to leave it lying there in the corner. I talked him into meeting at Bruegger's Bagel shop from then on, and when people walked by staring at his scar and wispy short hairs, he was to smile up at them as if to say, "I'm OK with it."

J: He did that?

A: He sure did. We met like that for five months. When he went in for the final check-up, he was ready for anything.

J: So what happened?

A: After a series of tests that lasted all day, the surgeon came into the waiting room and announced to us that he was giving him a clean bill of health. The stem had not grown, the healing was perfect, and he could go on living his life.

J: Wow! Hopefully, living life with a little less enthusiasm.

A: Amen. The next time we met, a few days later, he told me that he had determined how he was going to spend the rest of his life.

J: And?

A: He was going to the Seminary and become a preacher.

J: Really?

A: Absolutely. That was more than fifteen years ago. He now has his own congregation, as well as a wife and two sons, who more than likely will have an eye for the ladies.

J: What a story. What a story.

A: True.

Susan

A: I've been meaning to tell you about this woman I met.

J: Now that sounds interesting.

A: Very much so.

J: Let me see if I can stab at the basics. She's very attractive, younger of course, in our case everybody's younger, and she just may have got you wondering.

A: Right on all counts, but . . .

J: I'm listening.

A: Also very intelligent, great insights, extremely creative, intuitive, thoughtful, fun, has life in perspective.

J: There's no such woman.

A: I met her at the blood bank. When you finish giving blood, they make you hang around for 15 minutes to make sure you're not going to faint or make some kind of fuss. So we exchanged some pleasantries at the coffee table.

J: OK. It wasn't in some bar.

A: On the way out, we talked some more before getting in our cars and agreed to meet for coffee.

J: Ah-ha. Now it gets really interesting.

A: Yes, but not in the ways a devious mind imagines.

J: Oh. Too bad.

A: She is attractive, yes. Beautiful face, graying hair . . .

J: Nice smile, perfect teeth.

A: Yes, I noticed. But all that aside, it was those other qualities that sparked my interest. We met for coffee about once a month for over a year and exchanged insights on many topics, mostly relationships.

J: Really? That is interesting.

A: We'd start by selecting a word, one word, and give ourselves just five minutes to write down our thoughts. She had a lot of writing courses in her background. Then we'd discuss our thoughts.

J: What words? Give me an example.

A: At first she would have one ready. Later, I would. Like *family* or *marriage*.

J: Ah, I get it.

A: At Christmas, she gave me a wonderful present: a little book she had put together with one word on each page and several quotes from great writers or leaders relating to that word. Along with it was a little bag containing fifty-two little slips of paper, each with one word on it.

J: One for every week.

A: Right. I missed a lot of weeks, so it's taken me a lot longer than one year. But every time I do reach in that little bag and rattle my brain on another 5-minute exercise, I think of her.

J: She's gone?

A: Yes. I hadn't realized at the time that the gift would be so meaningful.

J: What happened?

A: Well, instead of meeting in January, I got a card with a nice letter enclosed, explaining that she was moving on and hoped that I would understand.

J: Wow. Where did she go?

A: I have no idea. I have assumed since that she was just moving on to other people.

J: That was a unique experience.

A: Yes. Exactly.

J: All the appeal of an affair, but on a higher level.

A: You could say almost a spiritual level. We spent a lot of time talking about the meaning of life and our purpose in life. She was always searching.

J: What was her background?

A: Are you ready for this? She was an attorney. She gave up her practice shortly after marrying another attorney. That was a while ago. She has a teen age son by that marriage.

J: Married again?

A: Right. To a man with two or three boys. Blended families, but she never seemed too happy about the situation.

J: Is that what you meant by searching?

A: I think so. I never ventured into it. Gave her plenty of opportunities to talk more about it, but I think I sensed a fine line in our relationship, and I didn't probe.

J: Kind of a respect.

A: Yes. And I think I felt that her instincts and outlook were better than mine. We exchanged openly, but we didn't offer advice. Does that make sense?

J: Yes. It sounds like a wonderful experience.

A: It was. I miss it. I miss her. She was a light in my life. Made me feel worthwhile.

J: Isn't it interesting how certain people come in and out of our lives? We wonder why. Is it really the hand of God? Are we supposed to be paying better attention? Is there something else we should be doing?

A: Yes. That's the feeling. She was wondering about life all the time. It was spiritual in the best sense. She had, like me, no use for religions as such, and she had a broken marriage and all that goes with it, but she was probably a great spiritual influence on everyone she met. Does that make sense?

J: She is an unusual woman, that's for sure. You were fortunate.

A: Still am. I have the book with all those words and all those quotes. She is still in my life.

J: You're a lucky man.

A: Don't I know it.

Does God answer your prayers?

A: Where do you suppose the Lord is with the state of the economy?

J: Probably shaking his head in wonderment.

A: We say that the Lord is with us in all things. How about the mess we're in?

J: It's our mess. He'll see us through. Give us the strength.

A: OK. He's not up there to solve our problems down here. Or is he? Does he wait for us to say enough prayers, and if we reach the quota, he steps in and fixes it?

J: You bring up a great topic. I always told people, when asked that, yes, he answers our prayers, but not always in the way we expected, or hoped for, but in his way and his time.

A: OK, let's say you're one of the 15,000,000 unemployed, and every night you fall on your knees and ask God to find you a job.

J: And nothing happens.

A: Right. Fourteen months go by. Now you pray that unemployment benefits get extended.

J: And they are.

A: OK. Did the Lord respond to the latter and not the former? Did he intend for you to suffer a little more? Get really desperate? Or weren't your first prayers good enough, and he wanted to get your attention?

J: Maybe all of the above, but maybe I shouldn't be praying for specific outcomes in the first place, just the strength and wisdom I need to get through this.

A: But scriptures tell us that whenever three of us get together, you know, wash our hands before meals, and all that, and keep the faith, our prayers will be answered.

J: In his way, in his time.

A: They left that out. You just added it.

J: Well, not entirely. Some of the scribes suggested that we pray for strength.

A: Then why are we encouraged to pray for specific outcomes? We pray for a safe trip or for Johnny to pass his exams or Carol to get off drugs.

J: Because we're human.

A: Which brings us back to God's will. We are encouraged to believe, in fact, we are taught to believe, that everything that happens is God's will. So are we praying to change his will? Are we presuming that if we are worthy enough or desperate enough or contrite enough, that God will hear our prayers and change his mind?

J: Well, that is the way most of us pray most of the time, and most of us don't really get serious enough about praying at all until things get pretty desperate.

A: You know how I feel about all this. Our problems on earth are man's problems, more often than not caused by man. They happen at random, and we all get a chance to experience them, because we have caused so many of them. No one escapes, and yes, God will provide the patience and courage and strength we need to get through them, but he is not up there orchestrating who gets cancer, whose kids are on drugs, whose marriages fall apart.

J: I'll go along with that.

A: I like to believe that God gave us an earth in perfect balance, with all the natural resources man would ever need, and all he asked was that we love one another as a way of showing our love for him.

J: And man has proceeded to screw it up ever since?

A: Right.

J: You started this by asking where God stands regarding the economy. We could ask as well where does he stand regarding the world situation; the earth, as you point out, man's abuse of those resources, the incessant wars and turmoil, Iraq and Afghanistan, Iran and North Korea; with China eclipsing America as world power, or better, world leader; with the loss of respect other countries had for us, and we ask, "Where is God in all this?" when we should be asking, "Where is man in all this?"

A: Oh, that's good! We carry on two useless "wars" that threaten to bankrupt us, morally as well as financially, to say nothing of the loss of lives, while we maintain our leadership in supplying weapons to all the countries of the world so that they can destroy their neighbors and often, their own citizens.

J: You skipped our leadership in greed. We think of Wall Street as the culprit, and rightly so, but the big banks throughout the world were in on the Ponzi scheme, major players in some cases. Now the workers, the middle class people throughout the world will have to foot the bill for one giant pay-back.

A: While China forges ahead in the growth fields, like solar panels, speed rail and education. They have the last laugh, at our arrogance.

J: Can you imagine how God feels looking down at all this?

Fading In and Out

A: You know how we laugh about walking into the next room to get our slippers that we're already wearing.

J: Oh my, yes. Or my *glasses* that I'm already wearing. Of course, as Jack Benny used to say, "I only need these for seeing."

A: Or getting distracted. Go out to get the mail and notice that you left the broom next to the steps and take it to the garage where you're reminded that you forgot to put the garbage cans at the curb yesterday but you spot the thistle on the shelf and figure you can make up for that lapse by feeding the birdies which brings you into the back yard where you see how the ivy is taking over the garden plot so you go to the shed to get a shovel and you glance back to see your wife on the porch wondering where the hell is he and where is the mail he went to get.

J: Or just forgetting names of people you see every day. The preacher is up there delivering the sermon and for the life of me I can't think of his name. I've only known him for years.

A: You've studied the brain. What is it? Are all those little neurons up there wearing out?

J: Something like that. Most studies show that they are making other choices, maybe parking some of what they consider less vital information back in the archives.

A: Like the computer?

J: Not unlike the computer. I'm sure there is a wearing away, but the indication is that the information is still there but tucked away.

A: Kind of like the boxes of old records I have in the attic.

J: Me, too. We can't let go. But there have been written many articles on how to stimulate the aging brain. Scientists have proven that the aging brain continues to develop, so we have no excuse for not feeding it.

A: Like how?

J: Well, one school of thought says to consider different viewpoints, different challenges for the brain. Studying a new language or sign language, taking courses in topics that are not familiar or comfortable, listening to teenagers!

A: Oh, man, that's another whole world.

J: Yes, and most of us throw up our hands as if we can't do anything about it. Maybe we should be studying the workings of the computer to see if we could possibly catch up to our kids' capabilities.

A: That hits home. That's a real challenge for my brain. I get so frustrated. I think I begin to get the idea in one small process and by the time I've figured it out, it's been upgraded to something better and faster.

J: I think we get credit for a good try.

A: Back to the brain, we see a lot more dementia or alzheimers or just plain losing it now that we're getting older and experiencing the signs.

J: Are we just naming it better? Did it always exist, but people just didn't live as long when we were young?

A: And does our speeded-up lifestyle today contribute to dementia, in other words, cramming too much stuff into our brains? Is there such a thing?

J: Are we programmed for just so much stuff, is that what you're asking? Are some brains able to handle more volume than others?

A: Yes, or are some small brains smarter than some big ones? The quarterback is a lot smaller than a three hundred pound lineman, but he's usually coherent in an interview.

J: I doubt if there are studies done on that one. But I remember that some studies did show that some brains can see the big picture better, in other words, put together the various pieces into a pattern or solution.

A: That sounds like the quarterback.

J: Maybe better said that they can zero in on what's important.

A: Then there's the crossword puzzle. My father swore by them. Or at them!

J: That's a great example. Something that makes the brain work, every day.

A: Which brings up another thought. Are today's kids spoiled by the internet? You know, all this information at their fingertips. They don't have to figure things out, so maybe they aren't using their brains as much.

J: Which could be countered by the fact that we didn't have as many challenges in our day. Things were a lot simpler then.

A: Amen to that. But are there answers to some of the basic questions about the brain? Let's take yours and mine. We think alike in a lot of ways, yet our early conditioning was quite different, almost totally different. So if the brain is ferreting away all the conditioners, can we assume that they somehow affect two different brains in the same way? Or that some conditioners have more effect on the brain, and that two different conditioners, like my having lost a business and family, your having lost the Jesuit life, could have a similar effect on our brains? Or am I confusing the brain with, say, an overall reaction that includes the emotions?

J: Well, I sure don't have an answer, except maybe "Huh? What?" and it would probably take an expert a day and a half to come up with one. We cannot begin to fathom the complexity of the brain, just the average brain, not the genius or brilliant scholarly brain.

A: Then we would have to get into how different people use their brains. The brain power of Harry Truman and George W might be similar, *but . . .*

J: Now, there's a topic.

A: For next week.

Sexual Abuse in the Church

A: Jack, I think maybe we should talk about all this sexual abuse within the clergy.

J: You may be right, but it saddens me. You have no idea.

A: I can only imagine.

J: What's our purpose? What can we accomplish talking about it?

A: Well, maybe just acknowledge its existence, its prevalence. Here's this vast conspiracy taking place worldwide, for centuries, and we live in denial.

J: There's no denying the denial.

A: And it is a conspiracy. Of the worst order. And magnitude.

J: Yes.

A: Here's all these fancy costumes and gilded robes in the Papacy of Rome, and a gentleman's agreement in the locker room to look the other way whenever one of them has a minor problem with the sexual urge.

J: You have a way of stating the case.

A: Well, the case has been buried by the Church that professes purity, and all the cardinals are hurt to think that their followers suddenly dare to question them.

J: As if this were just harmless little flirtations with young boys.

A: Right.

J: This time the problem is not just going away.

A: Exactly. The Church has already spent part of its dowry, million upon millions of dollars trying to appease thousands of men whose lives, and the lives of their wives and families, have been torn apart. God knows how many others have not stepped up to admit that they have been victims.

J: You're right. Maybe for the first time in centuries, the Church could be in financial trouble. Many of the schools are closing, churches are empty.

A: I'm sure there's plenty of money for the glories of Rome, but I think this giant hypocrisy within the church has come home to roost. Looking the other way has become one of the tenets.

J: But what do we do about it?

A: Yes. What do we do about it? We can see the Pope and his henchmen asking the same question, and coming up with the same old answer, "It will all blow over in time, not to worry. The sheep will continue to come to daily mass, or at least every Sunday, because they know they can't get to Heaven on their own, but only through us."

J: You paint a vivid picture.

A: I'm a little pissed off.

J: It's coming through.

A: You don't think the average Catholic is a little disappointed?

J: Of course I do. And the point you make about this blowing over has merit. The Church has weathered many storms in the past.

A: If they pay off enough people, this too will pass.

J: Most likely. And I hope so, because there are so many wonderful things about the church, and the religion.

A: Yes, but for people like me, those are undermined by actions. By the leaders who are supposed to be paving the way.

J: Maybe we could say it's because they are just humans, too.

A: Pretending to be one thing, and being another.

J: Yes. There's a lot of that everywhere.

A: But wearing the white collar to signify, to advertise, the fact that we are superior to the common man, because we can lead you to Heaven.

J: I knew this was going to make me uncomfortable.

A: That's not my intent. I think we have a right to expect our church to be open and honest. Trying to cover over a common problem that has existed for ages, man's sexual drive, and pretend that celibacy is the answer, has proven to be a little weak.

J: Absolutely.

A: You were one of the rare breed. It didn't even occur to you to step out of line. You were programmed from an early age.

J: Well, I had no interest in it, yes. I liked working with the nuns and women in general, but yes, I was programmed, as you say.

A: Or with the altar boys. Now, there's a group that got many a pat on the ass.

J: Back to the vivid picture.

A: But sex, man's sexual drive, has been something to behold from day one.

J: Back to Adam.

A: The Roman soldiers traveled with young boys, and they weren't just polishing their swords and shields. The old scriptures, written solely by men of course, treat women as vessels, depositories for the male urge.

J: Here comes the history.

A: OK. Fast forward to today. Where do we learn about sex? From our peers who are all screwed up, no pun intended. In our day, it was never discussed. You were supposed to learn about that stuff after you got married.

J: Today kids practice it in their own homes, because both parents are working, or in their cars, a lot of kids have cars. Some of them, twelve or thirteen years old, are into early sex.

A: That's mind boggling. Here's something that will affect them for the rest of their lives, that they aren't ready for at an early age, and the parents are kind of shrugging their shoulders, like there's nothing we can do about it.

J: Some would point out that playing with themselves maybe has a worse effect. Boys have been found standing on chairs with a noose around their necks and masturbating themselves to death.

A: Now you're painting a vivid picture.

J: You led me there.

A: You're absolutely right, and you segue us into another point. Families don't talk about sex. Schools have made an attempt, but then some parents howl in protest, insisting that discussing a subject so personal should be left in the home where, of course, it isn't discussed at all, or put off "until you get older."

J: It wasn't in mine, that's for sure.

A: I had three older brothers. You would assume that they would pass along some helpful hints. Blank.

J: They were waiting until they got older.

A: Right. I had a girlfriend, and I knew what it was like to get aroused. Often. But there was never any removal of clothes. I probably had as good an education in non-sex as you could expect.

J: I like that. I dated. Back then you walked them home from the movie. Maybe she'd let you steal a kiss in the vestibule. There was a curfew, and you'd better get her home from the movie by eleven o'clock.

A: And no empty house in those days. The parents were there. My girlfriend's parents were right there in the living room while we were necking in the sun parlor a few feet away. They knew we weren't doing our homework all that time.

J: They trusted you. That was a great lesson.

A: Yes. I often wished I had gotten to know her father better. I found out later that he had been one of the early cameramen in Hollywood and had married an actress who died in childbirth. He later married my girlfriend's mother.

J: Interesting, isn't it? We take older people for granted.

A: We know that.

J: Back to sex. Do you think we should have sex education in the schools?

A: It's an alternative, but so much depends on who is delivering the message. I think it's more likely that someone is going to come up with a package on the internet that can be accessed by parents smart enough to watch it with their kids and discuss it , you know, in segments directed to kids at different stages.

J: That sounds like a good idea.

A: Someone probably has it all figured out.

J: Wouldn't it be great if the church made it available?

A: We should live so long.

Transitions

J: I think we started all this by talking about what was happening to each of us in the years following that fateful 1968.

A: That was the most difficult time of our lives.

J: Right now the world is flooded with information. We are drowning in data, but we are lights out when it comes to the central issues in life, such as finding the meaning and purpose in our lives, managing relationships, finding peace and solitude, meanwhile acknowledging our limits and somehow living in uncertainty, or dealing with sickness, suffering and death.

A: And it all relates back to that turning point.

J: That's right.

A: I remember seeing this strange moving van backing into my driveway, like I was dreaming it, like it was in a movie, and they started removing the furniture. Anything of value, out the door. My wife had already taken the kids and headed South. I was left with one small file cabinet and part of a desk unit from my office.

J: Wow. My rupture came later. Get this: I had already obtained a dispensation from Rome, but the Cardinal in Boston would not have it delivered to me unless I agreed to leave Boston immediately. He demanded it. Here I was a tenured professor at Boston College, and now I was out of the Jesuits, out of a job and on the street. And I was broke.

A: I had a couple of months of wallowing around, myself, searching for support from Bishops and creditors and shrinks and a twenty six year old priest from the parish who obviously had some gender problems and was little comfort. Then one of my former clients, John Slaven at Volkswagen, a wonderful guy always ready to laugh, set up an interview for me in New York. They hired me, and you already know what happened after that.

J: In contrast, there was some light in my life in the years immediately following Vatican Two. I was a full time professor of psychology at BC, but I was also doing eight-day retreats for young priests, conducting conferences on religious education, and working with rabbis in interfaith programs and ministers in the Council of Churches. The best thing was being appointed to the Boston Theological Institute where I was rubbing elbows with leaders from Harvard and Boston University and learning how the Vatican Two bulletins were being accepted, or rejected, by the non-Catholic community.

A: You started to discover that there were other religions.

J: You laugh, but yes. Then I started working with the Confraternity of Christian Doctrine, and more important, the Catholic Family Movement.

A: I remember the CFM. I toyed with the idea of joining, but the wounds hadn't healed. I wanted no part of any religion, any church, any institutional bullshit of any kind.

J: They were wonderful. Here was a group in the church completely under the control of lay people. I was used to people saying, "Whatever Father wants to do sounds like a good idea to us." Not this one woman I remember, Ann Crowley, a firebrand with great leadership skills. Wow! A woman! Leading an organization in a Catholic church!

A: I wish I'd met her first.

J: That led to the Institute. I had met with the Dean of Deans at BC countless times, trying to persuade him to let me start a Summer Program ringing together theologians from all different universities to openly discuss the differences and commonalities of religions, to help bring about the unity, the peace that we were all struggling to find.

A: That would be a hard sell. Each theologian saying, "Ours is the only way."

J: He finally relented. We held our first Summer Program in 1970. That's when Mother Mary Hanley set the stage. On opening day, she had members of the staff meet each car and help carry the luggage of each participant, who were presented a printed guide containing information on the registration, the schedule of classes, restaurants in the vicinity, maps of the campus and greater Boston, and a list of places and events planned for the full eight days.

A. That's a real welcome.

J: They were knocked over. They were part of it right from the start. They not only attended the classes, they met with us at night for informal discussions. We had wonderful exchanges, sometimes lasting until ten o'clock at night. Those were long days, from eight in the morning, and I was right there with them, at every session.

A: I'll bet you loved every minute of it.

J: You said it. Most of the attendees were graduate students. At the end of the first week, they elected five of their members as Senators. The five divided the 145 participants into groups of thirty. From that moment on, and for the four years following, the program was in the hands of the participants.

A: You're probably going to tell me that's the way Socrates did it.

J: No, but yes. The success of the Institute was the best of times for me. It was the most significant contribution to the Jesuits, and the church, that I ever made.

A: And to the participants. Talk about reaching out.

J: But, at the same time the Institute was flourishing, I was beginning to doubt whether I could remain in the Jesuits.

A: At the same time, I was floundering. The job that would have enabled me to recover vanished after just three weeks when the owner had a heart attack. Meanwhile I had just remarried, on the rebound, and had signed a lease for an apartment that I could not afford. That prompted my first experience in driving a taxicab in New York City at night, the second shift, starting at four in the afternoon and ending at two or three in the morning. Then up and making the rounds to get a job, and later, just to get free-lance assignments, that would pay the bills.

J: When I was on the street, I ended up in the hospital. But let's go back to the taxicab. You're the first guy I ever met who drove a taxi in New York. I envy you for that.

A: Envy? Envy me? Are you crazy? I was desperate. I did that for months at a time, whenever assignments dried up, I'd have to jump in a cab to supplement my income. People think it's fun and exciting, but along about two in the morning and you're lined up outside a disco hoping for a fare to get you back uptown so you can take the bridge back to the depot in Queens, there you can walk back to the subway with your meager earnings, maybe fifty bucks for your nine or ten hours work, tucked in your sock, in case the muggers are cruising, then waiting on the subway platform along with a couple of derelicts, for the train back to the city, which at that time in the morning runs only once an hour, it can be a pretty humbling experience.

J: Especially if you're a little older. How old were you?

A: Like you, in my forties and fifties. But back to your crisis.

J: Well, I was overjoyed with the Institute, but deeply hurt by the slings and arrows I was getting from the traditionalists. I was praying like mad, the AA prayer was a big help, you know, "Grant me the serenity . . ." Pope Paul the Sixth had come out with his Encyclical, in that year 1968, upholding the traditional opposition to any type of birth control and harking back to the rhythm system, you remember that I'm sure . . .

A: I'm sure.

J: Restricting any sexual union to those days when the woman is biologically incapable of conceiving a child. Gone was the wiggle room we had as priests in the Confessional, that birth control was acceptable as long as the goal was not solely to avoid raising children, but rather, prompted by a health issue or to protect the marital relationship. It was a deeply personal decision between the couple and God.

A: But now that was gone.

J: Right, and I was torn. There was no way I could send people back to the rhythm system. The encyclical did me in. It was the tipping point, the symbol of where the church was going.

A: Without you.

J: Gone from the priesthood, the Jesuits, the Institute and Boston College. Years later, however, when BC celebrated its 200th anniversary, they honored 200 people who had made the greatest contributions over time, and I was one of them.

A: Terrific! On that note, let's close and head for the cafeteria. I'm interested to hear what brought you down to Raleigh, North Carolina.

From Priest to Prison

J: I know that we have talked about the effects of my leaving the priesthood, but I've been reflecting on it all this week. One effect led to my being banished from "the land of the bean and the cod, where the Cabots speak only to the Lodges, and the Lodges speak only to God." The other effect led to an incredible marriage and a chance to find the spirit of God alive and well in Raleigh, North Carolina.

A: That sums it up well. Now we fill in the blanks.

J: The Encyclical Humanae Vitae changed the course of so many lives, drastically. Only a system that was so centralized, legalistic, run by celibate male clerics, dogmatic and infallible, could make such a devastating mistake. Think of the guilt they heaped on good people throughout the world who then would be living in sin.

A: I remember.

J: It happened for one reason. If the church admitted that the teaching against contraception was a mistake, then the faithful could logically ask if the church might not have made other mistakes. The sheep might lose their belief in the credibility of the papal magisterium.

A: We couldn't have that.

J: What it meant for us, priests, was to live a lie. We couldn't believe what we couldn't conceive, and we could not conceive of Jesus preaching the Humanae Vitae. I made my decision to leave, I never looked back, and I never regretted it.

A: Did you find another kind of work right away?

J: Not right away. Like you, I had a bout with depression first. Then, a former student, Doctor Walt Cuskey got me a research assignment for six months in Pennsylvania evaluating treatments for recovering drug addicts, but when that grant dried up, I was back on the street. The good part of the story had to do with Mother Mary Hanley. She had also left her order and was working full time at the Helen Keller Center in Long Island, helping the deaf and blind. Meanwhile, her father, a former police officer in New York with plenty of stories to tell, died of cancer, and her mother was stricken with crippling arthritis. Mary and I were keeping in touch, because we had treasured an "Anam Cara" relationship over the years.

A: Right. Who was Anna Karra?

J: Anam Cara. That's Latin for soul-love. That's all we were allowed while in uniform, but after, we could become spiritual partners.

A: Which led to what?

J: A marriage, yes, but it took a while. What made it all possible was getting an offer to become the Chief Psychologist for the Central Prison here in Raleigh.

A: You're kidding. That's what brought you here?

J: Yes. I had worked with inmates over the years, and the prospect of devoting full time to making a difference in their lives down South really fascinated me. Eventually, I was appointed Chief Psychologist for the entire state.

A: What a wonderful transition, from priest to prison.

J: Yes, I used to tell people, "Watch out, I've been in the slammer."

A: What a great story.

Twenty years of turmoil

A: It's your turn. 1968 to 1988 again.

J: Oh, my, where to begin.

A: We've covered 1968 pretty well.

J: I had been giving eight-day retreats for young Jesuits, convinced that I could help bring together the teachings of the old Vatican One which dated back to 1870 and Vatican Two which opened the door to new thinking. They were being sent out into a Vatican Two world with an archaic Vatican One background. The old traditionalists were in a panic. Pope John the twenty-third embraced things like introspective self-study, evolution and renewal. Unheard of! He saw the church as the people of God, all joined together, not the huge Temple of the Bible or the fortress-like Church of Rome. Instead of being exclusive and secretive, it was becoming inclusive and open to scrutiny.

A: The big change for most of us sheep was the priest at Mass. He would now turn and face the parishioners, instead of conducting the entire process with his back to them, the constant reminder down through the ages that the only way to get to Heaven is through the priest and the hierarchy.

J: Perfect example. A major concession.

A: We watched them break the bread and pour the wine. Only the altar boys had been privileged before that.

J: Even the moral theology was changing. Instead of determining if a particular act was a mortal sin or a venial sin and applying the requirements of sufficient reflection and full consent of the will . . .

A: . . . "say ten Our Father's and ten Hail Mary's". . .

J: . . . in the new context, we determined if the person's fundamental choice was God and truth or turning away from God into selfishness, greed, cruelty or an unwillingness to forgive.

A: Pretty basic.

J: I remember giving a lecture at Boston University on this topic. As I finished, the audience suddenly broke into small groups and appeared to be very upset. I was a little upset myself until I learned that they had just heard the news that Martin Luther King had been killed.

A: 1968.

J: An added irony, we were in the same large classroom where King had previously studied for his doctorate in Theology, for three years.

A: That kind of connection makes you wonder.

J: Another incident like that. I was in Chicago doing a retreat at Loyola when one of the young priests asked if I wanted to come along with them to Franklin Park where the protestors were demonstrating at the National Democratic Convention. They were protesting the Vietnam War, as well as racial inequality, the FBI, banks, pollution and the general anti-establishment. The hate in the eyes of some of the protestors is something I'll never forget, and later in my room, I watched them being clubbed and beaten by the Chicago police. It struck me that these were Whites in the North, not Blacks in the South.

A: I wonder if the lack of protest today has something to do with the fact that the draft was sending all of America's young boys to Vietnam, but the so-called wars in Iraq and Afghanistan are being fought by Regular Army and reservists. Fox News, along with CNN and the networks keep us entertained first, to keep us buying products, and establish a comfortable mood of complacency throughout America.

J: I think you have answered your question.

A: Obviously, you were deeply affected by all that.

J: Yes. Those were troubling times, for me personally as well. Here I was traveling all over teaching young priests, encouraging them, persuading them to join me in bringing together the traditional teachings of the Church with the fresh thinking of Vatican II, and churning inside with the slings and arrows I was getting from the old traditionalists and the doubts and fears and concerns from these young men.

A: You were caught between the two Popes.

J: Yes, John opened the door and Paul was closing it. He slammed it shut with his encyclical Humanae Vitae in that fateful year, 1968, which upheld the Church's traditional opposition to any form of birth control other than , quote, natural family planning, otherwise known as the rhythm system.

A: I remember those days. No one talked about it, but a whole lot of people lost faith in the Church. We were having a tough time with our consciences, and the priests in the Confessionals were at a loss.

J: I was one of them. I had counseled thousands of troubled husbands and wives. I had always explained that they could use contraceptives as long as they honestly believed that it was necessary for the good of the children they were already raising or for health reasons or for the continuance of their relationship, you know, protecting that respect and trust.

A: That made perfect sense.

J: I came to realize that only a system that was centralized, legalistic, run by celibate male clerics, dogmatic and infallible, would make such a mistake. Imagine the sense of guilt instilled in people of good will who could not abide by the Encyclical and felt they were living in sin.

A: A sudden death and you go straight to hell.

J: Ironic. A celibate priest has to leave the order, because of a Papal blunder involving the union of a husband and wife.

A. Makes me grateful for my own union. Married a woman I hadn't seen for 40 years, inherited her five brothers, seven daughters, two sons, countless grandchildren, and most important, someone who has faced up to some of life's very difficult times, providing a great example for the rest of us.

Gotta be a better way

A: We laugh about your having spent eight years in the slammer.

J: I used that line a lot.

A: What did you take away from the prison experience?

J: Well, sometimes I think it boils down to just one thing. The reason so many men end up in prison is that they lost their dream.

A: How do you mean?

J: Just that. It's not a level playing field.

A: I thought you were going to say something about their IQs or living conditions.

J: That's a misconception. I found that the IQs were not much lower than the state's average. But the living conditions, yes, that played a part, a big part. When they were little kids, they had childhood dreams just like the rest of us. They wanted to be real heroes like they saw on television, not just the make-believe heroes, but teachers, doctors, nurses, mechanics, firemen, whatever.

A: But.

J: But when they reach the age of reason, say fifth or sixth grade, they realize that because of their home situation, their fathers missing, their neighborhoods, and the crowded schools, they probably won't make it as regular members of society, so they drop out.

A: That early? Fifth or sixth grade?

J: Most of them stay a while longer, of course, because some teacher or coach or custodian, maybe, made them feel worthwhile and important, that they could make things better for everybody when they get older.

A: When I think back, I remember that we had some good teachers that did just that in grammar school. I can still remember their names, including the gym teachers, Mr. Kenny and Mr. Kean.

J: You and I had the benefit of good example. Erich Fromm said, "Education is helping a child realize his or her potentialities," but the guys in prison saw themselves as failures early on.

A: Can the schools change all that?

J: Not in our lifetime, because the schools themselves would have to change. The whole system would have to change. Can the individual teachers make a difference? Yes, of course, but to reach more of the marginal students there would have to be smaller classes, and right now we're going in the opposite direction.

A: And the Paideia program would never happen.

J: Unfortunately. School is not just a building. It has to be a learning community, a total environment of discovery and sharing and experiencing.

A: That's an ideal, though. Teachers today have their hands full just keeping order.

J: Isn't that a crime! Students actually need *tutoring*, let alone smaller classes. So the teachers single out the students willing and anxious to learn, no matter what level they're in, and spend whatever time they can find to work with those few.

A: The rest fall by the wayside, like you say, and just drop out?

J: We say we can't afford more teachers and smaller classes, but just compare that to the cost of the prison system.

A: And the waste of human effort. All those people who could be   contributing to the common good.

J: We started out talking about the prison system, and here we are back at school.

A: Pretty closely related.

J: The word school, you know, goes back to the Greeks.

A: I didn't know.

J: Originally *schole*, and it stood for leisure time. The education of Greek boys, no girls allowed, was done by private tutors in reading, writing, arithmetic, singing, gymnastics, the total person. As the students got older, they would spend their leisure time listening to the discourses of learned men and that leisure time became known as school.

A: I'll use that somewhere to impress people.

J: As I just did. There were no graduations, because the Greeks never considered their education to be completed.

A: Before we get off schools here, how would you change the system?

J: Smaller classes, for one. Students need coaching. Maybe set up a network of associate teachers, retired people like us who could fill in.

A: That's a great idea.

J: Maybe once a week. That would help. I think students would benefit from experiencing their teachers and others discussing issues we are living with today.

A: Could be videotaped, then the students could discuss them.

J: Which brings up the seminar idea, the method Socrates started way back when. Not to get everybody to agree, but rather to get a shared understanding of the alternatives to be considered.

A: You said, "teachers and others." The others could be parents. Wouldn't it be something if we could get parents and teachers and students together, say one day a week, or even a month, to discuss an issue, like the *economy*. The old PTAs may have been a step in the right direction, at least getting the parents and teachers together.

J: Here the students would be discussing an issue that affects us all today.

A: Including parents would not be totally out of the question, because a lot of people today are working out of their homes, a good part of the time. Their schedules are more flexible.

J: We would be involving and educating everyone for the future. The economy is a good example. Another quote comes to mind. "Education is not the filling of a pail, but the lighting of a fire." I'm pretty sure that was William Butler Yeats.

A: That lighting of a fire is the dream idea you started with today, that the drop-outs lost their dream, their hopes for the future.

J: That's a fact.

Hell bent

A: I remembered another Stephen ministry experience I can talk about.

J: Shoot.

A: Here's the way I started his eulogy.

J: His eulogy?

A: Right. "Dutch was born about the time Pope John took over the Vatican. They both made quite an impact. He grew up just a few miles from the ocean, Wrightsville Beach. This one night he and his buddies, who got together all the time, long after high school, were out having a good old time at one of the local gin mills and were outside ready to head for home when one of them had a great idea. Let's run down to the beach and have a swim. Dutch was the first one in the water. Picture this big strapping guy, whoopin' and hollerin' and runnin' naked into the ocean. He's out there floating on his back, looking up at the stars while they're just getting their clothes off, when one of them has another idea, 'Let's grab his clothes and take off.' Which they did. Up over the dunes and out of sight. Dutch had to walk home five miles stark naked."

J: You told that at his eulogy?

A: It was fitting. They were always playing practical jokes on each other.

J: Some buddies.

A: They really were. They all kept driving up from Wrightsville, especially at the end. He had a rare type of leukemia, and he was wasting away.

J: Wow. Fill me in a little.

A: I'll go way back. He had a rough early life in rural North Carolina. His father got into the moonshine and disappeared when Dutch was about three years old. Two years later his mother died of pneumonia. His grandmother, a widow, took over and proved to be a tough caregiver. But loving, at the same time. She raised him and his older sister all through the school years. He was not a great student, but he was gifted with a brain for the technical. And he was a great athlete, from the time he was a little kid. He loved life, had close friends, both boys and girls, really popular. All-state halfback in football, scholarship to three different colleges, graduated with honors, all the time never giving up his wild side.

J: Sounds like a storybook.

A: He was for real. By the time I was assigned to him, he had a ten year old son by his first wife and was married to his second for about five years. He had had a couple of semi-serious girlfriends in college, and shortly after, and had met his first wife through his work. He had been hired right out of college by a firm in high-tech. They put him in sales right from the start, and he went gangbusters. When we met, he was traveling all over the world, setting up programs, doing well financially.

J: Then?

A: Yeah, then. He'd been feeling sluggish, totally unlike him. You know, this guy was high-test, all-out, full-blast. Suddenly, no energy. Series of tests. They find out he has a rare type of leukemia. Cancer. In his blood.

J: The worst.

A: Right. He goes through the chemo, radiation, the range of treatments for months. They keep him alive, but all the time he's getting weaker. And you can imagine what that was doing to his psyche.

J: Was he in depression?

A: Definitely, but he wouldn't admit it. He was down, but he was all fight. He wouldn't give up. One of the few positives was his relationship with his son. He had more time with him, he was a great example for him. It was sad for me to see them walking together toward the end, Dutch getting weaker all the time, finally with a walker.

J: Wow. That's heart-breaking.

A: The last resort was a stem-cell transplant.

J: Replace all the cells?

A: I'd never experienced someone going through that. It was unbelievable. Like something out of a science-fiction movie. Here's your close friend, once a big hulk of a man, the ultimate athlete, now a pale, frail body strapped to this huge apparatus that seemed to be hanging from the ceiling. It's shaking him violently. The sound of it alone was deafening. Boom, boom, boom. He looked ghost-like, a lifeless body being kept alive in a torture chamber.

J: I can't imagine.

A: All I could think of was that he was already dead, that his soul was already in heaven, and that they were keeping the remnants of the body alive to demonstrate that they could do it.

J: Whew.

A: I had been alone in the chamber with him when his wife came in. I had been praying hard, you can imagine, my head in my hands, and of course I didn't hear her. She took my arm, and we stood like that, both of us trembling and sobbing.

J: Wow.

A: Finally, we left the room. She asked me what I thought, and I told her. She agreed, and went into the room where the doctors were huddled. They agreed, and it was all over.

J: Wow. That was some experience. I feel like I was there.

A: All his buddies were at the wake *and* the worship service. They loved the eulogy.

Relationships

A: I'm wondering if maybe relationships, when all is said and done, are what life is all about.

J: That sounds like something we should talk about.

A: There are so many different kinds of relationships.

J: Yes, and they are the most important part of our lives.

A: We take them for granted mostly, get involved in our work, how we make our living, and the relationships simply develop.

J: I think that's true. Starting with the basic family, the relationships develop naturally, dependence of the kids on the parents through various stages until they get on their own.

A: The different relationships between family members, where one of the kids is wild and the other mild.

J: The fact that family has a whole different connotation today than it did when we were growing up. Today it's an occasion when they all have dinner together. With us, it was a given.

A: Which suggests that our relationships today are with *things*. Cell phones, I-pads, tablets.

J: The cell phones and the internet enable us to connect with more people, and faster than we ever dreamed, and I suppose we could say that is relating.

A: Kind of quick-hits, staying in touch. Yes, but.

J: But what?

A: Well, I guess it's relating. I had more in mind that we talk about personal relationships. Like between man and woman.

J: Oh? How much time do we have?

A: Whatever it takes. Supposedly, it all started with Adam and Eve. Let's get rid of the apple and the serpent and pretend that Eve wasn't a bad girl and that the two of them got it on naturally and we're off to a peaceful start.

J: Bliss.

A: The Creator must have had that in mind. Man was endowed with the appendage and woman with the vessel, and they shared a mutual respect for each other.

J: It was a good plan.

A: Right. Let's skip the free will at this point and skip head a few centuries to today's relationship between man and woman.

J: Ah-ha. Not so good. You're going to say that the mutual respect is gone.

A: Something like that. The equipment we were born with became labeled as sex, and nice couples did it but didn't talk about it.

J: Well, today we have marriage counseling and it's more open.

A: Yes, but. Husbands and wives even today do not discuss their sex lives openly and honestly.

J: That's a broad statement.

A: OK. *In my experience* dealing with men going through marital problems and witnessing the attitudes and reactions of couples, sometimes outright embarrassment when the subject may be brought up, or even alluded to, usually in a humorous way, maybe an off-color joke. I'd say that it's the rare couple – in our times, for sure – that continuously or *continually* would be more accurate, express how they feel about their sex contract.

J: I'd have to agree with that, stemming not just from the confessional, but the many meetings with couples in my practice.

A: I think it goes beyond the sex life. Because husbands and wives don't talk about sex, that sets the precedent for not talking about anything that might be deeply personal or might offend the other party.

J: Bingo. I think you've got it.

A: A few smart people get some counseling before marriage, but I'd like to see a course on *relationships*, the whole magilla, introduced in grammar school. The kindergarten teachers get them started, but I mean when the kids are a little older, fifth or sixth grade, a course featuring Nouwen's respect and trust.

J: If we could only get Paideia off the ground. That would be a great topic for discussion. Today, bullying is getting some attention, and rightly so. The conditions that contribute to that kind of behavior, a fractured home life with both parents working, or worse, with the breadwinner now unemployed, or neither one working, those conditions are going to be ever more relevant.

A: And teachers are dealing with too many students in a class, and activities for the kids are being cut back and often eliminated.

J: That's a relationship in deep trouble. Teacher and student. Teachers have all they can do to cover the curriculum, sometimes just to keep peace, let alone develop any kind of relationships with kids who need counseling.

A: Kids who need some kindness, maybe, some encouragement that could make a difference in their lives.

J: Which could make a difference overall, in everyone's life. In society.

A: I'd like to think there's an opportunity for more emphasis on relationships, maybe first in schools, but somehow on television, not the preachy evangelists, but a meaningful series on getting along with one another, as individuals, as communities, as workplaces, as *countries!*

J: Dream on. But there certainly is a need. If only to answer all of this texting and social networking which is creating a whole new system of connecting, but leaves a question about relating. A lot of it unhealthy connecting.

A: It's overwhelming. Everyone walks around with a phone glued to their face, or worse, while they're driving with one hand, or with their elbow, so they can drink their coffee at the same time.

J: But you're right about the need to reach young people.

A: And the parents. Wouldn't it be wonderful to get them together in some kind of a program that would catch on and spread.

J: As a nation, we seem to be lulled into a feeling of helplessness, as if there is nothing we can do about our problems.

A: Too bad. I guess it goes right back to the family.

J: Yep. That's where relationships start.

Prayer 101

J: Last week when you started asking about prayer, that really got me thinking, and so I did a little homework.

A: Ammunition, I bet.

J: No. Not exactly. But I looked up in the scriptures what guys like Matthew, Mark . . .

A: . . . Luke and John.

J: . . .and a lot of others had to say about prayer, and then ask for your comments.

A: Shoot.

J: Matthew says we can pray without saying a word.

A: I'll buy that. It's the thought that counts.

J: Right. Next: Job says God does not punish us when we question the value of prayer.

A: I'll buy that one, too. I don't think God is in the punishing business, in the first place, and I do think he would like us to question a lot of what the ancient writers said about anything.

J: OK. Here's one from Proverbs and Timothy One: our prayers please God.

A: I don't know. I think he likes to hear from us. Send him an email once in a while.

J: This isn't going the way I thought. Here's one from Matthew, Luke, Ephesians and Colossians: we are to pray for our friends and our enemies.

A: I have trouble with the last part. Are we to pray for our enemies to succeed or get hit by a car?

J: Change their ways, I think. We all have trouble wishing them well. Here's Matthew again and Thessalonians: we are to pray against evil , you know, deliverance from evil and for its defeat.

A: Well, that's a big one, for me. I believe evil is part of our makeup. Inside. I don't believe in the Devil, either. Satan. I think he was manufactured. And you know how I question taking the Our Father literally, as in "lead us not into temptation" and deliver us from evil" as if the Lord is up there parceling it out.

J: There you go again. But you do pray against evil in your heart?

A: Yes. I pray for strength to overcome my lustful thoughts at age 84. They're mine, alive and kicking. My responsibility. I think the Lord wants me to deal with it, and he will help me if I ask and really mean it.

J: I don't know if your interpretations of the Bible will get you to Heaven, but they certainly are interesting. How about Timothy two: we are to pray for our leaders.

A: Amen to that one. Obama is negotiating us into one hell of a mess. With a Congress that is hopeless. There's a real challenge for prayer.

J: You'll like this one. Matthew makes the point twice, Mark once, and Luke three times: our prayers are not to impress people.

A: You're right. That's a given. The Lord hated hypocrisy.

J: Here's another given, from Acts: we can pray when we are suffering and even when near death.

A: Yeah. I think we all get religion when we're in deep soup or on the way out. I think our best prayers are when we can just talk to God. Tell him how confused we are, make that how confused I am, and how easy it is to do something wrong instead of right. How difficult it is for me to shake my past, the shame and guilt, and look at my sculpture of Jesus without wincing.

J: You said before that you simply pray for strength and his grace, his blessings.

A: I say that, but I find myself praying for specifics. I soften them by asking the Lord if he might "look in on" my brother while he's fighting cancer. Not a real, outright specific.

J: In other words, give your brother the strength and grace.

A: Yeah. Like that.

J: It sounds like you're saying that what is happening may be God's will, and you don't want to question that.

A: Yes. Or that I know he will handle it in his own way.

J: And on his schedule.

A: Right. Praying to an Almighty God is not easy for us sinners. I would like to think of Jesus as a very special friend who knows me better than I do and is always ready to bail me out with another advance of grace.

J: I like that. I think he would, too.

Power of Prayer

A: Today I thought we might say a prayer for each other.

J: Oh, I like the sounds of that.

A: It's a sneaky way of saying that I want to ask you about prayer.

J: Shoot.

A: Why are some prayers answered and some not?

J: They are all answered, but sometimes, most times, not in the way we asked, and not always on our schedule.

A: That kind of sums it up but doesn't get you off the hook.

J: Hmmm.

A: So, in other words, our prayers that aren't worthy end up in the waste basket.

J: I don't think the Lord hits the delete button on any of our prayers. He responds to them appropriately.

A: Of course, from his point of view. We don't have that option. From our point of view, the prayer wasn't answered. So why do we pray for specific things.

J: Again, because we're human.

A: We're told, in the scriptures, that whenever three of us get together and agree on the gift we seek, that our prayer will be answered. Doesn't that suggest that we get the gift?

J: No, not necessarily. Look at it this way. In a family, the son asks his father for a shiny, new car for his 16th birthday, knowing full well that his father will consider that not a good idea. But if he asks the father to work on a project with him, the chances are good.

A: Or, be careful of what you ask for.

J: Some of that, yes.

A: I ask for specifics all the time. Yet if someone were to ask me, I would say, no, I know enough now simply to ask for strength. Strength to get through some difficulty, and grace, because I know I'm not much of anything without grace. But the fact is, I do ask the Lord to keep my brother's cancer in remission, and my close friend's, and to look in on my care receiver's marriage, and so on and so on.

J: And if that doesn't happen?

A: There was a time I blamed God. I'd get pissed off. During my years of feeling rejected, and rejecting him, I ranted, shaking my fist at the ceiling of my one-room rent-controlled apartment.

J: Feeling that he regarded you as unworthy?

A: Words to that effect. I was one troubled puppy.

J: In other words, if your prayers weren't answered, it was because God deemed you unworthy?

A: Something like that. I had stopped praying. For years. I accepted the fact that I was unworthy, yes. Guilt took over.

J: How did you pull out of it?

A: Oh, that's another story. Do we have time for it?

J: We'll make time.

A: Well, after about fifteen years living apart from God, I just naturally turned it all over to him. I was working a second job on the graveyard shift editing legal briefs, eleven p.m. until seven a.m., down on Wall Street, and I would skip lunch at three a.m., who wants to eat lunch in the middle of the night, and that enabled me to leave a half hour early, and I would change into my shorts and running shoes and jog back uptown, about five miles, to my apartment. One day, after months of this routine and out of nowhere, I found myself saying Hail Mary's as I was jogging along. I hadn't done that since standing in the chow lines in the Army. I didn't know why I was doing it, but it felt right. Then I began saying, "Jesus, mercy," with every footfall, and that felt right. Then one day I jogged right past my building and went another eight blocks to a little chapel I had been in for a friend's funeral. I kneeled in front of a statue of the Virgin Mary. I didn't say anything, didn't attempt a prayer, just kneeled there. That became part of my routine. Then one day one of my brothers called from Maryland to ask if I remembered a guy named Bruce Mundie. You know the rest of the story. He was my current wife's little brother when we were going together in high school, and we reconnected.

J: Wow. That is a story.

Q & A o n F a i t h

A: Today I have a bunch of questions.

J: I'm all ears.

A: My wife has a ready answer for everything, but I'm interested in yours.

J: Shoot.

A: Who are you? Who should you be?

J: Easy. I'm a child of God. And I have been given gifts that I'm supposed to use.

A: Great. You must have rehearsed that.

J: Many times.

A: I'll turn the questions around. How about our self-esteem? Can we really like the persons we are, instead of beating ourselves up because of past sins and mistakes?

J: God doesn't make trash, and he accepts us just as we are. You know the expression, "God hears the prayers of the repentant sinner."

A: Great. I feel better already. But why am I here? Is there a reason for my life?

J: To help others, sometimes to serve others. You're a Stephen minister, so you know all about that one.

A: Well, I accept it now as my purpose in life. But something else troubles me. Like, considering the present, how can we face the future without hope and despair?

J: Whooeee. Trust in God, I guess. Our generations have dropped the ball. We've advanced like crazy in technology and speeding everything up, but we have turned the world economy inside out and we can't seem to govern ourselves peacefully.

A: And we're fast approaching the capability to virtually wipe each other out. Trust in God is right. OK. Why is there evil in the world?

J: God will have to answer that one. Why is there evil in our souls? Gets us back to why is there free will?

A: Why do we fail all the time?

J: Because we're human. It's part of living. And not all the time. Sometimes, for sure. I like the expression "fall forward." When we fail, we ask for grace, for strength, to fall forward, pick ourselves up and get on with it. We fail because we are human.

A: My father rarely gave his sons any advice. He always said that we learn best by our mistakes. But along with failing, how about guilt?

J: That's a big one.

A: We've covered the Nun's mantra about going to hell if you fart out loud.

J: I didn't hear that one.

A: It was loud. You weren't listening. But *guilt*. Man, I wake up mornings, or half awake is more accurate, thinking about all the times I did something that hurt someone I loved.

J: I hear you, but I think we all experience some of that. We did it, it's done, and most times there's nothing we can do about it. The conditions have changed, and time has done some healing, but we can't undo what's been done.

A: Yeah, and sometimes the loved ones are no longer with us, which somehow adds to the guilt.

J: You wouldn't be suffering guilt if you didn't care so much. Look at it that way. Some people can hurt others, continually, and just go on their way.

A: If we're the ones getting hurt, how do we forgive?

J: The other side of the coin. Well, I honestly don't know. Do we ever really forgive someone who betrays us, or do we just say so and harbor the feeling? If someone we love really lets us down, it's a bitter pill to swallow.

A: I don't know which is worse, being the betrayer or the one betrayed. With more than half the marriages broken, there's probably a lot of betrayal going on.

J: You can bank that.

A: Why do we do things we regret later on?

J: Because at the time, we were tempted or we feared a certain outcome or we simply made a dumb decision.

A: At the time, that's the key. If we had a chance to do it all over again, but if the conditions were the same, we'd make the same dumb decision.

J: Right. We spend a lot of time living in the past. We have to learn how to accept the fact that we're only human. Learn the lesson and get on with it.

A: We're learning. Finally. At this ripe old age. How come we have to grow old?

J: Yeah, just when we're starting to get things in perspective.

A: Hope we hang around a while longer.

J: Hope is the thing with feathers . . .

A: . . . that perches on the soul . . .

J: . . . and sings the tune without the words . . .

A: . . . and never stops at all.

Competing in the Universe

A: You know how I go on about the idea that there might be other earths out there in space and the Creator is up there watching to see what happens?

J: Oh-oh, here he goes again.

A: Well, guess what? There's an article in the Times about a new satellite observatory zeroing in on 400 stars that have characteristics similar to our own.

J: OK, the Lord could have knocked those out in no time.

A: Yeah, but if they have characteristics similar to ours, they could have *characters*, similar to ours, roaming around the same way.

J: I suppose that's a possibility.

A: You bet it is. We know there are thousands of earths out there in space, some 200 light years apart. The article says it would take a rocket traveling about 39,000 miles an hour about 300 years to reach another planet.

J: That's a long trip. Farther than from here to Asheville.

A: So why don't we suppose for a minute that those 400 are also inhabited with human beings just like us, and they all started out at the same time with the same natural resources, but, of course, in different places.

J: OK, they're all examples of the Lord's creative bent.

A: Not just a *worldly* competition, but a universal one.

J: I feel this one coming.

A: Right. He gives mankind, and womankind, *free will* to see what they do with it.

J: He knows all things, so he knows what they will do with it.

A: Maybe and maybe not. Maybe God wants to run a pilot program with the 400 before he underwrites the big corporate Launch of the Several Thousand.

J: Maybe now you're having too much fun.

A: No. I respect his ability to do anything He wants. It's not a competition to sort out the weeds, like if the humans screw up, the whole planet goes to hell. No, it's to see which ones, if any, would use the natural resources to create their own version of heaven on earth.

J: I like that. We have a few natural resources left, so maybe there's hope for us here on our earth.

A: Not much at the rate we're going. If we were really concerned about the world our grandchildren will inherit, and theirs, we would make damn sure we had some intelligence in our Congress instead of short-sighted dimwits who view any issues, or possibilities, in terms of how much the lobbyists will pay for their vote.

J: Now we're getting down to earth.

A: Let's dabble some more in the stellar system. There is so much good in the world, but the bad guys get all the headlines. So, here you are in the Garden of Gestafus. You're looking around for our version of Eve, so you can get this population thing started.

J: Good move.

A: There are no snakes on Gestafus, and no apple trees, either. Along comes this knockout woman and you fall in love. She doesn't have to tempt you. It's natural that you jump in bed.

J: So far so good.

A: Along come the children, the happy family. Nobody kills his brother or sister. They're all happy on the farm and loving one another.

J: When does this free-will thing kick in?

A: That's the point. The free will is used in positive ways, in helping one another.

J: But no, free will gets us in trouble. We get tempted, we lust after women and money. We make all kinds of mistakes.

A: That's here on earth. We're talking Gestafus now.

J: So there's no evil, no sign of Satan?

A: Right.

J: So you're saying Satan is an invention.

A: Of course. On Gestafus, everyone is content with what they have. God is alive in their hearts, because he is the great provider.

J: Are you suggesting that we could have some kind of heaven here on earth?

A: I'm suggesting that there could be several versions of life in a pilot program of 400 earths.

J: You'll admit that's a little way out?

A: Maybe light years way out, but perfectly possible. Compare it to what we've been taught. You could write a better Genesis. There we have Eve as evil woman, the first manipulator! You can be sure that a man wrote the first version of the Bible. And a serpent? That's reasonable? Cain and Able, jealousy and murder? That's family? How come no daughters?

J: Well, it could maybe use a little editing.

A: Amen to that.

J: You're crazy, but you give us lots to think about.

What happened to the Economy?

A: I suppose you were checking the Dow this morning.

J: The what?

A: The Dow. You know, all your investments.

J: They're in the piggy bank.

A: Great article in the Times, now you're going to ask me who wrote it and I forget, but he made the point that everybody checks the Dow when they should be checking the GDP.

J: I know that one. Gross Domestic Product.

A: You get an A-plus. He points out that the markets haven't been restored because the government's money drops are being used to skew the asset prices, whatever those are.

J: and we're being skewed in the process?

A: I think that's his point. He says the best way to gauge the real economy is the GDP, because it's a combination of three things we can all understand: consumption, investment and government spending, like the stimulus. Actually four, I think, because he includes exports and imports.

J: I think I'm getting confused.

A: Well, me too. But it's easy to see that the unemployed aren't spending as much as they once did, and the great unwashed middle class is sinking, so consumption is down bigtime, and that's what drives the economy.

J: Comes right back to creating jobs, something our Congressman know nothing about.

A: Right. Consumption is the big player in GDP, like 70%, and it's going downhill.

J: Investments likewise, I'd guess.

A: Right. I think that was 10%, in the same direction. Companies are sitting on their profits. Everybody's happy up top, but they aren't taking any chances with anything that might create new jobs.

J: And government spending has been a real wash. The stimulus was too small in the first place, and it all went into the same old pockets.

A: I don't know about the imports and exports, but we can see in every product we pick up that they aren't made in the good ol' USA.

J: One of these days, we've got to start talking about something pleasant.

A: You're right, but if only enough people could get a handle on where we are and what needs to be done.

J: We're dreaming, but let's say you're Obama or a top legislator with some intelligence, if there is such a thing, what would you be recommending?

A: I'd rather be Paul Krugman, and I'd be recommending that we create some jobs to get the economy healthy, get people back to work and have some money to spend. Until that happens, we're headed for a real Depression. We've blown trillions in Iraq and Afghanistan in senseless wars where we have accomplished nothing, just built up this immense deficit.

J: Yes. Put it in terms of a family, where the old man hits the bottle, goes on a tear, blows the money they had saved for the kids' education and puts them deep in debt.

A. Exactly. He has to get his life back in order, get back to work, and somehow work their way out of debt.

J: But how do we, now, create jobs?

A: Well, it isn't rocket science. For one, the nation's infrastructure needs a lot of work, and not just roads and bridges. The bridges are bout to fall down, like the one in Minnesota, but we are way behind China in the growth areas. Rapid transit, for example. Here in Raleigh, we're congratulating ourselves for talking about it while China has a whole network in operation, 300 miles of speed rail running from the coast to Beijing with plans to extend it across Europe.

J: I read where they offered to connect our West Coast. Of course, that would be a real embarrassment.

A: There's electric cars. Ford and some of the others are beginning to catch up, but there's a whole network of charge stations to be put in place. There's energy and the whole green effort which has been stalled effectively by the Big Power companies, but it's a field that could be creating hundreds of thousands of jobs.

J: I know where you're going with that. Get the big companies sitting on their profits to loosen up and risk some of that on new ventures.

A: Absolutely. Technology and the entire information world is moving so fast that it is eliminating jobs. That's why we start with the infrastructure. Like the old WPA in the last great Depression. Get some of those fourteen to twenty million people back to work on something tangible. Just releasing subsidy money to the states results in money going into the same pockets, as you just said.

J: What else would Krugman do?

A: I think he would rein in Congress somehow, make some real changes. Like one-term only and no fat pensions for life. I think he would release a record of where the millions of lobbying money goes, how K Street is the strongest arm of our government.

J: Would he go after the military?

A: Absolutely. He'd point out how Eisenhower saw it coming and warned us, this is Eisenhower now, the four-star General who led us out of WWII, telling us that the cozy military-industrial cash cow was already out of hand.

J: We didn't pay attention, because there was, and is, so much money to be had.

A: But to get back to the positive, there is a lot of opportunity for jobs in a field that may not be glamorous but will continue to grow: the health field. We right away think hospitals, but that's the tip of the iceberg. The population will continue to grow older, think all of the Boomers and their needs increasing every year of their lives. Retirement homes, entire communities moving people from one stage of disrepair to the next and finally out.

J: We're experiencing it, my wife and me, but we're going to stick it out here in our home as long as we can.

A: You can afford to bring the services in, so you are creating jobs.

J: Where else are the jobs?

A: Let's stay with the health field for a minute. Think nursing, physician assistants, nurse practitioners, nursing homes, dental technicians, anesthesiologists, medical equipment, data – what an opportunity there, to mine all the data that could prevent illnesses, home healthcare – like you have here, patient transportation to keep old people alert and moving.

J: That's a start.

A: Education, another area the Tea Party wants to scuttle. You spent many years advancing the Paideia program. Just think how the nation would benefit if you had the money to expand it into the mainstream, along with other programs that would keep our students ahead of the world. We know that just the opposite is happening. The computer has leveled the field.

J: But the opportunities are there, it isn't rocket science.

A: Amen to that. The media, again, has to take some responsibility for the nation's apathy. We're getting news as entertainment. Selective news.

J: The media can say that they're urging people to keep right on buying. They're supporting *consumption!* Speaking of consumption, let's go get lunch and talk some more about what can be done.

Putting problems in perspective

J: We were talking about Stephen ministry last time and got depressed with the marriage state.

A: We make a lot more headway with the other problems, even sickness, I mean serious illness, and deaths.

J: Things like job loss?

A: That's a big one, and it won't be going away

J: Kids on drugs?

A: At an early age. And early sex. That's an amazing thing to me. In our day, getting a feel through three layers of clothing was considered making out. The Youth Director at church is amazed as well.

J: They talk about it there?

A: Yes. He says, "Hey, it's happening. It's a problem. We talk about it, you bet." That doesn't put an end to it, but talking about it enables most of them to stay out of trouble.

J: Or at least not get pregnant?

A: That, too. There's a whole different lifestyle today. A lot of the kids come from broken families, we've talked about that, single parents, both working, some kids have their own cars, plenty of free time after classes let out, they have allowances, there's no supervision, no discipline, they get in trouble.

J: Along with crack and pot and booze.

A: And now they get caught up in the seamy side with all this social networking. We read about how they spread some really awful stories, or photos, of some girl who happens to be going with some guy who one of her rivals wants to make out with.

J: I read about a couple of those.

A: You can imagine how often stuff like that is happening. At an early age. I'm talking about grammar school in some cases. I remember, vividly, my introduction to the younger generation when I was a substitute teacher in New York City. For a short time, believe me. Picture this. Big public school, between classes, halls jammed with hundreds of kids shouting and shoving, bell rings for next class, nobody pays any attention, the din is unbelievable, shouting and squealing, screaming and laughing. I manage to get a few into the room, Study Hall, but this mass of humanity is like animals surging back and forth. There's this one group, close by, surrounding a really hot looking girl with low cut blouse, a tight, short skirt, the uniform, you know. She has them enthralled with her adventure with a high school hero I guessed. These are seventh-graders I'm talking about. Finally I get this group to make their way into the room, where she promptly sits on top of a desk and continues the spellbinding with all the squeals and screams of an adoring audience. I put up with this for a few minutes and figure if I can get her to take a seat, the others will follow. So, threading my way into this scene, I approach her with that suggestion. "Fuck you," she says, loud and clear, with hardly missing a beat, to the squeals and delight of her entourage.

J: You got the idea that you were out of touch?

A: It's a different time we're in.

J: How did you handle it?

A: I lost it. I was so mad, I got in her face and said, "You sit down at this desk, like a normal person, or I'll smack you one you won't forget and drag you to the Principal's office by your hair." She gives me a "Hymph," but she took a seat and the room was quiet for a few minutes.

J: Makes you wonder what it's like *today*. That was what, twenty years ago?

A: More. Time flies. Seems like yesterday. But can you imagine trying to be a teacher today in schools like that, especially with the pre-teens?

J: A lot of them from single-parent homes, broken families. It's so hard to get through to them. Even connect with them. The teachers I've talked with say, "There's no time to deal with the trouble-makers, to really help them, just send them down to the Principal," knowing that half the time they go home instead, or worse, just meet up with their buddies on the street.

A: The fact is that our young people today are going to face challenges like we've never seen, especially in the workplace. People without an education are going to be lost, because most of the labor-intensive jobs will have disappeared, replaced by robots and technology.

J: Walk into a big manufacturing plant today, and you're struck by how few people there are. It's all conveyor belts and robotic welding.

A: Getting back to Stephen ministry, job loss today provides a lot of assignments. There are fourteen million people out of work, probably more because nobody is creating jobs. Companies are making profits, big time, but they are not investing, and when and if they start, they will invest in capital equipment, you know, more robots, that eliminate jobs.

J: You said before that companies aren't hiring employees even when they have a need, that they hire on a contract basis, six-month assignments where they don't have to pay for health insurance, 401-Ks, retirement benefits, none of that.

A: We've belabored the point, but if you were running a company, you would be sending the jobs overseas, too, and you would be right, in order to stay competitive.

J: So meanwhile, the number of people out of work keeps on growing, and we keep on providing unemployment benefits, five hundred bucks a week. How long can we do that?

A: The sad part is that most of them do not understand what is happening, that their old jobs are never coming back. They're gone forever, replaced by technology or people overseas. They are not willing to face up to the fact that they have to study the emerging marketplace and find a niche where their skills and experience, and obviously some new training, can be applied.

J: That's a mass of people, and growing.

A: Working with them one-on-one in Stephen ministry, we're able to help them get the problem in perspective, but you can imagine how being out of work affects the entire family. It's whole new way of life, a whole new ball game.

J: Broken families?

A: Absolutely. The head of the house, the traditional family provider, is collecting unemployment and floundering around in part-time assignments, at best. Some quit and become Mister Moms, watching their self-worth go down the tank. Others are not that fortunate and take up with another woman, seeking solace.

J: You're describing fourteen million people?

A: Maybe more, if we count people on the fringes. Now add serious illness, deaths, kids on drugs or anorexic or totally screwed up in the social media mix, the usual peer pressures, anger management, and the everyday relationship problems, and you can see that people in the program stay busy.

J: It's a great program.

A: We get a great return on our investment. Just being there for someone in trouble is a great reward.

The Good Listener

J: Tell me more about Stephen Ministry and how you counsel people in trouble.

A: Well, first, the ministry is spelled with a small *m*, not a capital. We're not ordained Ministers by any means. And we don't counsel people, at least we are not supposed to.

J: Sometimes you cross the line.

A: In my case, several times, many times, but we do receive training before we're let loose on some poor soul in deep soup.

J: What kind?

A: Mostly on how to be a good listener. You know from your own training how important that is.

J: Amen.

A: And not just in the Confessional.

J: I hear you.

A: Most of us half-listen, forming our response before the person finishes his sentence. Or more likely, *her* sentence.

J: Oh my. Yes.

A: In Stephen ministry, men are assigned to men, women to women.

J: What kind of trouble are they in?

A: What you'd expect. A pretty good range of problems, starting with the marriage relationship. More than half the men I've been assigned to were struggling with that. It's more than coincidental that my first three assignments were with married men. The first was thirty-five years old, the second, thirty-six, and the third, thirty-seven.

J: That told you something.

A: Stands to reason. More than half the marriages in America end up broken. Right here in River City.

J: Seventy-six trombones led the big parade . . .

A: With all the pious Bible Studies, and Gospel studies, you can look down your row when you're in church and count ten people, and you know that five of them are experiencing a marital problem at that moment.

J: What, even in church?

A: Well, they probably left the problem in the car, but it's there waiting.

J: I'd guess it's more like seven out of ten, with maybe only two out of the seven seriously working at it.

A: You've put your finger on it. They stop working at it.

J: Couples today get caught up in what I call the TV picture of marriage; you can easily back out if you aren't getting all the goodies available to you in the commercials.

A: TV doesn't show the effects of a break-up, particularly on the kids. Think about it, all those young people experiencing "blended" families. The blending is often anything but.

J: Forcing the kids to bear the brunt. Suddenly the parents they loved, who loved them, no longer love each other.

A: They're in different homes now, or apartments, with different partners, who the kids are supposed to accept without question. Meanwhile the kids are exposed to the sniping of the parents with their former partners, creating a rift that's confusing and painful to them. The kids regard the whole thing as betrayal, which it is, and they no longer trust either parent.

J: You bring it home. This is happening in more than half the families in America. Pretty soon the kid living with his parents will be the odd-ball.

A: How do you explain it? Is it a whole combination of things? The influence of television, and now the internet, the philosophy that you can have it all, the fact that the Boomers have grown up with it, they don't have to sacrifice, serve in the Army, or stay with a partner if someone else comes along who is more attractive?

J: All of the above. We've let the Murdochs of the world twist our thinking. As long as it makes money, it's OK.

A: Our lifestyle makes a mockery of Nouwen's version of a good relationship, based on respect and trust.

J: That goes out the window when a couple breaks up.

A: It's seen as some outmoded way the previous generations locked up the couple for life. I know a few couples who have stayed together, and I have to admit, some of them, probably most of them, seem very tired, unhappy, resigned to it. Again, maybe it's the influence of television, the philosophy of you can have it all.

J: Something like that. A combination of things.

A: I find that I get down at times, envying others who have the wherewithal to travel to Europe or just travel more in general to be with my extended families and friends.

J: It's so easy to feel sorry for ourselves today. We get bombarded with a need for more. What do you tell these people you get assigned to?

A: It depends. Usually, they are already deep into the split by the time they ask for help. It's too late to encourage them to work on saving the marriage. They have already decided to abscond with their new love who is probably absconding with his new love, both convinced that "The kids will adjust. They'll be fine."

J: So how can you help?

A: Well, you try to get him in perspective. If he's the one left behind, if the wife is the one absconding, he has a real trial on his hands. He is not only deeply hurt, he has to witness, to *experience,* the anguish of his kids. He is the one who has to provide the real meaning of family, and home. Their mother is already settling in with the new stepfather. Dad here is expected to be a good sport and help her move some furniture.

J: Is it that bad?

A: Many times. If the shoe is on the other foot, if he is starting a new life with the woman he has been running with, sometimes literally, running in the park in the early mornings, then he is the bad guy having the book thrown at him by her lawyers. Getting him in perspective is like pulling him out of a deep well.

J: Where do you start?

A: Well, our mission is get our care receiver in perspective with one, himself; two, the people around him; and three, the Lord. Sometimes in reverse order.

J: That's a tall order. Especially if he is the one walking out, because he's probably walking out on the Lord at the same time.

A: Right. Expecting the Lord to wait outside for a while. Those are the toughest ones for me, because the damage to the kids lasts a lifetime, *their* lifetimes, and sets the example, that they can walk out when things get tough.

J: Maybe if the kids are older, say in high school or college, does it ever have the reverse effect, that they vow to have a lasting relationship?

A: I hope so, but the precedent has been established, and don't forget, the younger generation has been raised in a *you can have it all* lifestyle. If we keep going the way we're going, the lasting marriage will be an oddity.

J: Be a lot of old people, like us, living alone in a nursing home.

A: They call them retirement communities today.

J: We could have our pick of all the hot chicks there.

A: As if we could do anything about it.

J: But I get the point. Have you found that the spouse who has been left, the one walked out on, is the one left with the heavy load of raising the kids, whether it's the wife or the husband?

A: Yes. It's tougher on the husband, because first he has to keep his job, which is tougher now because he's emotionally drained and not as sharp meanwhile he has to run the household and keep track of the kids with baby sitters and trying to leave work early to get his son to soccer games or his daughter to volleyball or whatever.

J: And the kids have their own peer pressure and take the old man for granted.

A: You got it. "How come we can't have this or that like when Mom was here?" And they get tired of going from one household to another for a week at a time or weekend schedules made difficult by Mom and the new husband running off to the beach.

J: They no longer feel important. Or loved.

A: Exactly. Difficult enough to adjust to the pressures at school, especially because kids can be cruel, and now they have a very unsettling home life.

J: No wonder they react in strange ways.

A: It's not a pretty picture. For me, the marital assignments are the toughest, primarily because by the time they ask for help, they are already into the divorce. There is nothing we can do to save the marriage.

J: So you are there to listen, enable them to unload?

A: Mostly, yes. We can help guide them, because we've been there before. In my case, directly, and we usually get them back in the hands of the Lord, to some extent, anyway.

J: But you can't save the marriage.

A: They have already made that decision. That's the depressing part. It's possible that down the road a few will see the light and get back together, but I haven't seen that happen yet.

J: Are some of the other experiences more rewarding?

A: Absolutely.

J: Let's talk about one of those next time.

More Slammer stories

A: I like your line, "Watch out for me, I spent eight years in the slammer." Did you ever go back, once out?

J: Yes, but only in emergencies. Sam Garrison and Mrs. Bass were no longer there.

A: What kind of emergencies?

J: Well, there was a lock-in not long after I left. That's when a few inmates corral some of the staff and hold them hostage. They had six of our people in the records department with knives put up to their throats.

A: That's scary. What happened?

J: Fortunately, nobody got killed. Eventually the inmates gave in. But I got the call to come meet with the people who had been held hostage. Scary is right. You're locked in with the prisoners, and you don't come home to supper, you don't come home the next day, and you know you might not come home at all. Some of the prisoners are not mentally stable, and killing people is not something beyond their regimen.

A: Man, that's an experience you wouldn't soon forget.

J: Exactly. Most of them never came back to work, a couple stayed on. That takes a rare brand of courage.

A: Whew.

J: Another incident happened after I retired. They executed one of the prisoners, a woman named Thelma who had been charged with poisoning her husbands, two or three of them. But she had made a genuine transformation in prison, and she had become a wonderful guide and example to the other prisoners. She was beloved by the staff and everyone else. Well, you can imagine, she had been sentenced to death. The death chamber hadn't been used for a woman in the previous 40 years.

A: They went ahead with it?

J: Yes. They had to. There was no choice. But here were all these people who had come to know her and love her. Really. I got the call to come meet with each one of them, to help them adjust. It was really post-traumatic stress disorder, which was one of the skills in my bag as a psychologist. At one point, I had taught police how to handle stress.

A: You were able to meet with all of them, individually?

J: One by one. That's the only way. There was this one big guard, probably six-five, two hundred eighty pounds or more. He sat down and within minutes he was crying. He said, "I used to play Santa Claus for them, and she would come sit in my lap." The chaplain told me, "After the execution, my wife and I went to New York. The hotel was near Times Square, and I couldn't sleep at night. I went to the window and looked out and there was Thelma sitting in a rocking chair, rocking."

A: Oh, my God.

J: Each one had a story like that. The death penalty is wrong for a lot of reasons, but one stands out in my experience: you can't pay someone to kill someone on a legal basis, like the electric chair, without its having a profound effect on others. Many others.

A: The prison system needs an overhaul, in your eyes.

J: For sure. There's never enough money to do things that make sense. Just enough to keep them all locked up and off the street.

A: You've said that you did make some headway.

J: Yes, thanks to a great extent to Gordon Smith, who at the time headed up the Governor's Crime Commission. It was his vision that a few bad guys could prevent a lot of young people from ending up the same way. So we set up a program where I would train a few inmates, who had earned credits for good behavior, how to get on their feet and talk to an audience. Some of them went back to the high schools they had attended, imagine the impact that had, because they would be describing what it was like to be in prison and how they got there. Once they had done it a few times, they became almost articulate, and they were dynamite in the Q&As.

A: Wow. That was a great idea. Is it still going on?

J: As far as I know. We reached young people all across the state. It was a win for everybody involved: the inmates, of course, in gaining their confidence, which was a real plus for them once they got out and were looking for work; the kids in school who got the message straight from people who never did get the message; the city cops who escorted the inmates, in overcoming the fear and distrust and anger toward them; the school administrators who experienced a change in attitude within their entire student bodies.

A: Kind of put the missing respect in perspective.

J: Yes. It proved to be a great way to get the message into the community.

A: No wonder you miss being a part of it.

J: I thought about it, long and hard, but I got another offer I couldn't refuse.

A: Ah, I sense another story coming up.

Back in the Slammer

A: When you were talking about the prison experience and the impact that the warden, Sam Garrison, had on the inmates, you also said something about your secretary, that she was somehow almost as valuable to you.

J: Oh, yes.

A: Is there a story there?

J: Oh my, yes.

A: So?

J: In my first few days there, in fact, during my first interviews, it became increasingly apparent, to me, I didn't reveal my apprehension, but it was real, that I didn't know the first thing about the prison system.

A: And there you were in charge of a bunch of young psychologists.

J: Exactly.

A: Who may not have been too well informed, either, in the beginning.

J: Exactly. So when I started interviewing people to hire as my secretary, I was hoping to find someone already in the system.

A: Right.

J: One candidate was what you might expect, a really good-looking young lady, in her young twenties I'd guess, with little interest in the inmates or anything else other than a steady job with little responsibility.

A: How good-looking?

J: Not that good-looking. I kept asking the Superintendent if there wasn't a secretary around who had been there a long time, even twenty-five or thirty years, who knew something about the system. Finally, reluctantly, he said,

"Well, yeah, but you wouldn't want her."

A: Oh-oh.

J: "So, who is it," I said, "Maybe I would."

"Well, Mary Bass, he said."

"Why wouldn't I want her?"

"Well, they call her Mrs. Prison. She'd have you for breakfast."

"Where is she?"

"She's up on the third floor, probably typing, facing the wall."

"What was her job before?"

"She was assistant to the Superintendent for three different men."

"Then why is she being treated that way, *Mrs. Prison?*

"Well, because she once wrote a letter to a judge that offended him."

"I want to talk with her."

"You'd be crazy to. That's crazy."

They all said I'd be crazy if I talked with her. But I did.

A: I'm all ears.

J: I told her, "Mrs. Bass, I've got a problem. I've been hired to do a job, and I don't have the savvy to do it. They tell me that you have had more experience than anybody in running this department in the Division of Prisons. She acknowledged that was true. Then I added that they told me that I would be crazy to talk with her, because she would have me for breakfast. She had to smile, and said, "Don't you pay any attention to those people."

A: That was the start?

J: Yes, but the smile vanished, and her eyes were like beacons as she stared into mine, "Do you get to work on time, do you? Do you stay late when it's necessary to get the job done? When they call me Mrs. Prison, it's because I learned everything from one of the three bosses I had. The second one was never near as good and the third rarely showed up. So I had to take responsibility for administrators who wouldn't take responsibility for themselves. Are you one of those?"

A: Wow. She let you have it.

J: I'll say. My stomach was churning. But I told her, "Mrs. Bass, I intend to work my head off to make a difference here. I'm responsible for the young psychologists working here, and together we're responsible to the inmates. If we're going to make anything happen, I have to understand how. How are we restricted? How are we supported?

A: And how did she react?

J: She didn't say anything for what seemed like an hour. Just kept staring at me, as if deciding whether to believe me. Finally, she said, "Fine. I can help you, *if* you mean what you say."

A: Wow. That was the real beginning?

J: She was incredible. She was a walking history of Central Prison. At first, she was trying simply to be a secretary, waiting for me to dictate letters and the like. So I sat her down and explained that I wanted her on a different level, discussing each issue with me, coaching me in the ins and outs of the politics, the hierarchies that exist in every kind of institutional setup. She was terrific. She responded like someone released from prison herself.

A: The smile returned.

J: Yes! And the respect, both ways. It turned out to be one of the most rewarding experiences of my life. Because we were able to achieve some things that never would have happened. Together, we were able to add programs that made life worthwhile for the inmates and gave new life to the psychologists. They were excited to see things happen, suddenly everybody loved coming to work.

A: That's a statement.

J: Everybody loved coming to work? Yes, imagine. People who previously had dragged themselves to work, hating the drudgery but putting in their time, because it would look good on their resumes. Now they were part of making a difference in people's lives. Inmates who had given up on life, who had no hope.

A: Wow.

J: We would stay late at least one night a week. The psychologists, just to talk over what we could make happen. And we were getting noticed. I was getting invited everywhere to speak about the changes we were making at Central Prison. It was building, you can imagine, over eight years?

A: Why did you leave?

J: Oh, that's another long story. I was overdoing it, and I had a heart attack. Mrs. Bass found me slumped over my desk, and the prison doctor got me to the hospital in a hurry. Triple bypass, and a long recovery.

A: That is another story.

J: Probably leading to more.

Picture yourself in prison

A: Tell me more about your prison experience. I can't imagine what it was like to be working with inmates all the time.

J: Well, most of the time I was working with the psychologists who were working directly with the inmates, but I made it a point to meet with the most troublesome or special cases.

A: That's what I wondered about.

J: The most troublesome were often the lifers, the ones without any hope at all.

A: I can't imagine how that would be.

J: Depressing. Just unbelievably depressing. There's really nothing you can offer them. Some can barely read. Those are the most difficult, they just give up; then some get violent, you know, out of total frustration.

A: But do most of them settle into some kind of rehab program?

J: Yes, thank goodness. The psychologists do a wonderful job, under the most difficult conditions. Some of the inmates are really grateful and appreciate that someone cares and is trying to help. Some make the most of the time they have on their hands, get into exercise programs and study groups.

A: Bible studies?

J: A lot of that. A good percentage draw closer to the Lord, understandably. Some can quote Bible passages better than a preacher.

A: So there's hope for some.

J: Well, yes. But I'll tell you what I found to be the most meaningful influence.

A: What's that?

J: The warden.

A: The warden?

J: Yes. Sam Garrison, one of the most impressive human beings I ever met. Young, only in his thirties, and big, six foot five or six and built like a bull. He had the respect of the inmates, but not out of fear. He knew how to relate to them. They knew he cared about them and would always be fair and direct and honest.

A: That's not the way we picture a warden.

J: Right. In the movies, the warden is an unbending tyrant. Let me give you an example of Sam. One hot summer day, he said, "Jack, I want you to go up to the fourth tier and tell me what you see." I did, the inmates who were allowed outside their cells were sitting, in their shorts, on the cement, sweat pouring off them. Sam said, "What would you think if we brought them some cold lemonade?" Which he did. He sent gallons of it up there.

A: Meaningful, like you say.

J: There were 107 men on death row. I was really taken with them, because they were the easiest to manage. They gave you no problem and were grateful for anything you did for them.

A: How many inmates, total?

J: Almost fourteen hundred. Central Prison was like a Bastille, a dismal, foreboding place, built after the Civil War, walls four foot thick, barbed wire, scary. If you were to visit there, you would go through a series of rooms, alone, four walls, thick metal doors slammed shut behind you, hidden cameras exposing your insides and outs. They call them sallyports.

A: Built after the Civil War? Really? Over a hundred years ago?

J: Yes. When we were young, years ago, they would take whole busloads of school children to visit prisons, sit in the electric chair, scare the hell out of them.

A: Make sure they understood how important it was not to end up there?

J: Yeah. I can't say enough about the psychologists we had, so dedicated, trying so hard to keep the inmates somewhat sane in a system totally geared to dehumanize.

A: *Geared* to dehumanize?

J: Simply because it's the cheapest way to keep uncontrollable people off the street. Some, many, should be in mental hospitals, but that costs more. Everything else costs more.

A: That's what it boils down to? Money?

J: Absolutely. I was telling you about Sam. This one time he gets a call from a Sheriff in a nearby town, saying we've got one of your inmates who escaped, we've got him surrounded, but he lets us know he has guns, maybe a bunch of weapons. Sam says, "OK, but don't do anything until I get there." So he goes about 90 miles an hour to get there, and they tell him he can't go in, and he says, "I sure as hell can. I know him. He'll listen to me." They tell him, you can't go in there, we won't let you." Sam says, "You can't stop me. Get the hell out of the way," and walks up the long front yard, shouting "Mickey, put down them damn guns and open the door!" The guy says, "Is that you, Sam?" And he says, "You know damn well it's me." So the guy puts down the guns, and Sam walks him, not to the State Police car or the local police, but to his prison car. They are all staring at this picture and ask, "Aren't you going to cuff him?" Sam says, "Why should I cuff him?" So Sam drives him back to prison, giving him a big lecture on the way.

A: It's a wonder they didn't stop for coffee on the way back. What a story.

J: There are lots more.

Basic instincts

A: Like you, I go around the house all the time talking to myself, aloud, or talking to inanimate objects. Kind of a running commentary while carrying out the basic activities.

J: You're saying I do that?

A: I get that impression, yes.

J: You're right.

A: My wife gets a little annoyed with mine. So yesterday when I entered the bathroom, I made sure she was within earshot.

J: Oh-oh.

A: I addressed the commode with, "OK, now, brace yourself. This will all be over in a few minutes."

J: Oh, that's good.

A: She cracked up.

J: She had to laugh. Is this leading up to something?

A: Of course. I thought we might spend a few minutes talking about basic instincts.

J: Instinks?

A: That, too. She always reminds me to turn the fan on.

J: There were no fans in our day. No exhaust fans, anyway.

A: Even the ones today don't exactly clear the air in a hurry.

J: Depends on how heavy the air is.

A: Have you ever been confined in a small space with several others, like in the army, well, maybe you were, when you were in training for the Jesuits.

J: We were usually in dorms.

A: Well, in the Army we had six men crammed into a small hut surrounding a pot-belly stove, and the air was often blue with basic instincts.

J: Grin and bear it.

A: More like grit your teeth. There was an innate acceptance of the fact that you had to be ready to vacate the premises on a moment's notice.

J: You should have kicked out the culprit.

A: We were all culprits, Army food being what it is.

J: Well, this is a subject indeed worthy of our deep consideration, and you don't seem ready to change it.

A: In my father's shop, when I was a kid, the men were all sitting on wooden stools as they lettered the signs.

J: Oh-oh.

A: You got it. Reverberations accompanying the fireworks. An ongoing contest ensued as to who could create the most resounding response.

J: What was the prize?

A: Recognition, man! Admiration. This was man at his best.

J: I can see that you aren't through with this.

A: Iggy was the champion, probably because his wife gave him a steady diet of onions and garlic in his lunch pail.

J: This does trigger a few embarrassing episodes. I remember delivering a speech before an august group of corporate big shots on a crowded dais. I was silently praying, while I was expounding, that the men sitting alongside me wouldn't notice.

A: All the time knowing that they had to be aware.

J: Unmistakable. There's always that tell-tale trace.

A: I remember trying to impress my high school girlfriend and her younger brother by demonstrating the tough exercises the coach made us do at football practice. Legs up and over, and just as the feet hit the floor, the stomach let go.

J: Boy, were they impressed.

A: She played that back, "up and over" for a long time.

J: Imagine trying to impress the nuns when you aren't in full control.

A: Like when you sneeze, do they say, "Bless you, Father" when you fart?

J: Under their breath, maybe.

A: There are times though, seriously, when a fart isn't funny.

J: Here comes the philosophical part of the discussion.

A: OK. I said seriously. When husband and wife use it as ammunition.

J: Now we are being serious.

A: Yes, just for a minute, I promise. For the husband it's power, demonstrating who's the boss here. The louder the better.

J: It says, "I don't need to show any respect for you."

A: Right.

J: Even if she has one ready, she won't respond in kind, she won't lower herself to his level.

A: You got it. See, that's serious. It's an expansion of the one-ups and put-downs.

J: She might save one for bedtime, speaking of one-ups.

A: Silent but deadly.

J: I think it's time to put this subject to bed.

The Past is Dead

A: In my half-awake moments lying there in bed in the early morning, where I'm usually treated to a parade of stupid mistakes I've made in my life, this morning, somehow, a vision of Disneyland appeared.

J: There's a call for a psychologist.

A: Or a dream analyst.

J: At least. Where did it go from there?

A: I'm not sure. There was a small artificial lake and one of those little trains, you know, pulling people around, and a roller coaster in the background, and then a dark, theater-like exhibit room with a big screen, more like I'd remember seeing in Disneyworld in Orlando.

J: Cross-country dreamer. I have my own recall of Anaheim.

A: I guess it got me thinking about Disney himself, starting with cartoons and ending up with huge fantasy parks.

J: Do you want to expand on that half-awake time? Do you really start the day with a review of the mistakes you've made way back when?

A: I'd like to say no, but yes. Maybe not every morning, but yes, most mornings. I'm happy to get the hell out of bed and splash cold water on my face.

J: Well, I understand that.

A: I'm grateful that I have one more day to try to do something worthwhile.

J: That's the good part. The bad is still in your subconscious.

A: Right.

J: Your sub-conscious is stuck in the punishment mode. It wants you to suffer some more. Guilt was really imbedded in your youth.

A: Maybe it was my Mother always saying, "What will the neighbors think?"

J: Or maybe the nuns, you've mentioned it many times, that you're going to go straight to hell for all the wicked things you've done.

A: Right. But I don't blame the nuns. I take responsibility for my mistakes, but they are really difficult for me to comprehend at this point in my life. How could I have done such stupid things?

J: That's hindsight. At the time, you were probably escaping or compensating.

A: Yes. Compensating, more likely. I was mad at the Lord for a long time, and maybe that made it easy to look for an out.

J: I think talking about it, like you do every so often, is helping you shake it. I think those half-awake moments will disappear once you start accepting the fact that you are doing a world of good right now. You're using those mistakes in helping people you meet with to avoid them, avoid the same kind of mistakes you made.

A: Or live with them. Put them in perspective.

J: They're history. The past. The Lord didn't make them happen. But he will use them.

A: That's the good part all right.

J: Anaheim reminds me of a low point in my life. With a happy ending.

A: Shoot.

J: I was scheduled to speak there at a big conference. Hundreds of big shots from the corporate world assembled to hear how their companies could actually make more money by treating their employees better. I was on the panel of psychologists and other freaks who were delivering the message.

A: I can't wait to hear it.

J: Well, I got the shakes. When I suddenly realized that I would be a member of a panel composed of these renowned psychiatrists and was slated to deliver a 45 minute lecture, I got really scared. I was intimidated by the CVs of these people, and I reviewed my speech, full of my usual asides and witticisms, and I thought dear God, what am I doing here?

A: I know the feeling. I bet you were ready to turn tail and run.

J: Exactly. I didn't have time to change the speech, and I was in no condition to do it, anyway.

A: So what happened?

J: Fortunately, my good friend, another priest whose parish was in Los Angeles, had come down to see the show, in this case, see me fall flat on my face. Well, anyway, he took me by the arm and walked me around Disneyland for two hours, bolstering me, finally restoring my confidence and enabling me to face the music.

A: You got through it?

J: I knocked 'em dead. Got a standing ovation.

A: They loved your witticisms.

J: It was a turning point. I knew from then on that I would never be intimidated, either by an imposing panel or by a corporate audience.

A: That is a happy ending. Or really, beginning.

J: Yes!

A: Makes me think of so many times when we anticipate the worst, and it turns out to be a triumph.

J: Right.

A: One comes to mind. I remember back when I had my own business. We had a client, Fenestra, that had been huge in the steel window business, but was getting killed by aluminum windows, and we had come up with a marketing and promotion campaign to rescue the firm, and I was slated to present it to the Board of Directors in Chicago. We were in Buffalo, remember. You can imagine, for days we're frantically putting together the presentation, I hop on a plane at six a.m. on a freezing cold winter morning, knowing that with the one-hour difference in time, I can just make it to the meeting by nine o'clock. We're barely in the air when the stewardess announces that because of the weather, the arrival time will be delayed by approximately 20 minutes to a half hour. And I panic. I envision this staid bunch of wealthy men looking at their watches, and I start reviewing all the glitches in our presentation.

J: I get the feeling.

A: We're late, just like she said, and I'm running through O'Hare. Jump in the taxi and start thinking of what I'm going to say, how I'm going to cover the bad start. The driver gets me there in a hurry, but he has to let me out next to a frozen snowbank. Only room for the door to open part way. There I am with both hands full, trying to squeeze through, one leg still inside, I'm stretching the other one out to get a foothold, when I feel a tug and a sudden draft. I had ripped the bottom out of my pants.

J: Oh, man.

A: Well, that gave me my opener. When I got to the meeting, I started by taking off my suitcoat and bending over to show them that I busted my ass to get there.

J: What an opener!

A: They loved it, and they loved the presentation.

J: Another happy ending.

A: We've had lots of them, haven't we?

J: Amen

A lesson in learning

A: I was reading about this magnet school in Hartford where eighty percent of the enrollment is Black and Latino and they had zero dropouts last year.

J: Really? Wow, that's meaningful.

A: And every graduate was accepted at a 4-year college.

J: They're doing something right.

A: The principal said that college acceptance is their goal.

J: That should get a lot of people thinking. You know, magnet schools got their start as a remedy for racial segregation. This takes it to a new level.

A: What's the main objective now? I always assumed they were designed for the brighter students or the ones who wanted a special curriculum.

J: That's part of it. They do attract students who already have in mind the kind of field they might like to work in, and they can get a leg up with special courses.

A: I probably would have studied art and ended up on the street, same as now.

J: Maybe, but maybe you'd have been a wealthy doctor or lawyer.

A: Never. But I did start out in pre-law, thinking I'd make a good trial lawyer like Gregory Peck appealing to the jury, but I got a whiff of having to wade through reams of legal briefs and switched to Economics.

J: That was your major? Business?

A: Yeah. I didn't know I would have to take Statistical Analysis. I held the record at the University of Buffalo; failed it twice, dropped it three more times. I'm not good with numbers.

J: I can see that.

A: Kept me from graduating. Thirty-five years later when I was in New York, I went back to night school and got my BS in Communications.

J: That figures.

A: Right. But this whole education thing intrigues me. You were involved in the Paideia program, too. How does that fit in?

J: I thought you'd never ask. Paideia, pronounced Piedayuh. It's a wonderful program, founded back in the '80s by Mortimer Adler. It was set up to help students accomplish three things: become good citizens, earn a decent living, and lead a good life.

A: Terrific.

J: Instead of lecture-type learning, the teacher at the head of the class and the kids listening and memorizing and taking tests, there's more of a seminar, more training of individual skills.

A: How do teachers find time for that, with the size of the classes increasing even more?

J: That's a fair question, and it does call for a teacher with more than average skills. It's a combination of increasing the students' recall; coaching, and then the seminar dialogue, to strengthen the students' understanding.

A: Sounds like a tall order.

J: Paideia, most people pronounce it pay-dee-a, it's pie-day-uh, the program has a great record in making a real difference. It's located right here at UNC and run by a great guy, Terry Roberts. We became good friends. I remember they did a study of nine different types of schools in all different states across America, all at-risk schools, where the students had been behind academically. After Paideia, they were consistently above other schools in their districts and across their states. above proficiency across all grades, for several years. Providence, I remember, my home town, was way above.

A: Are the techniques adaptable for the public school?

J: Some already are, but it's up to the school boards in most cases, or the state, or federal regulations.

A: I let the word didactic slip by, as if I know what it meant, but I'm interested in that coaching of skills, seeing as that is what I have been doing most of my life, but I didn't know it had to be intellectual coaching.

J: I think that's probably the way the academe would describe it.

A: Would one of the skills be *communicating*, especially on their feet? They get comfortable talking to one another in a seminar setting, chairs or desks in a circle, then it's easier for them to talk to one another on their feet. But what are they talking about?

J: Ideas, mostly. Concepts, values. Not names and dates and formulas.

A. Ah-ha. Now I see. We get them to exchange their thoughts on issues. They learn from each other, as well as the teacher.

J. Right. He, or she, becomes a facilitator.

A. Or referee.

J: It can get pretty noisy, but mostly there's a lot of good-natured kidding.

A: Makes me want to go back and start all over. Now that I can pronounce pie-day-uh.

Communicating 101

A: Today I'd like us to talk about one-ups and put-downs.

J: I like the sound of it.

A: It's what I've found that most married couples do.

J: Ah-ha.

A: Some, early-on in the relationship, but mostly it's a progression which finds its ultimate perfection in later life.

J: This is great. This is familiar ground.

A: Yes, we all practice it. And you have probably counseled people in it.

J: Yes. But too often it's ingrained.

A: Instead of cultivating the habit of talking to one another early-on in the relationship, really establishing an honest exchange of feelings . . .

J: That's heresy!

A: . . . as in the wife revealing what the husband says or does that makes her feel good, not just bad, and he reveals what she says or does that makes him feel good, not just bad. Rarely does the husband risk saying anything.

J: He holds it all in.

A: And, eventually, explodes.

J: And she is surprised at his outburst of anger and informs him that he should do something about it.

A: You've been there, with your patients.

J: More than once, believe me.

A: Same for me in the caregiving program. I've been assigned to more than 30 men over the years, and more than half were having a marital problem.

J: In keeping with the national statistics on broken homes.

A: So instead of being open and honest with each other, couples engage in an ongoing competition of who can one-up or put-down the other.

J: Well put.

A: Yeah, the put-downs can be devastating.

J: One-ups are less caustic.

A: The galling thing is that women seem to be so much better at put-downs. And, after a certain point, you know, they collect. You end up feeling like you should go off in the woods and die like a dog.

J: You're worthless.

A: Right.

J: Why in the world did she ever marry you?

A: Right.

J: She should have married Johnny Jones.

A: You'll never amount to anything.

J: Why are you taking up space in this world?

A: You got it.

J: With most couples, the competition begins when the honeymoon period ends, when the love conquers all gives way to how do we pay the bills or the new baby introduces a whole new set of conditions.

A: Suddenly they are partners in a marriage venture. The wedding was a mirage.

J: Right. Now, they're competing. It's you did this or didn't do that, and he says that's because that's your job, I'm doing my job.

A: And the jibes and jabs get worse as they go along. What's really galling, like you say, is that women seem to be so much better at it.

J: Yes. The jabs increase, and the severity, right along with the stages of married life. First, there's the honeymoon period where there might be a hint, shared jokingly, that either party might have a fault. Then comes the reality, that they're in this together, and the other one isn't pulling his load, or hers.

A: And she's pregnant.

J: That's the start of the second phase. She's carrying the load, literally, and she starts to let him know it.

A: It only gets worse as the number of kids increases.

J: Right. Now we're into the adolescent years. The pace of the one-ups and put-downs increases with the number of kids and how close they are in age, you know, the kids are all going through different stages, too, and the oldest have probably joined in the competition by now.

A: Then the empty nest?

J: Right. Now the parents have the field to themselves again, and they are free to slam home the digs without being overheard.

A: And they start growing apart.

J: They have been growing apart. Now they become aware of it. They openly criticize each other, find fault, operate from the negative.

A: We've all experienced it. We see it in others before we see it in ourselves.

J: Amen to that. We see it in restaurants. We see it in dinner parties or family gatherings where it is apparent that a couple is no longer happy with one another. They don't have to say anything, we know.

A: They're waiting until they get back in the car, then the carping starts up, along with the engine.

J: So many people spend their late years in bitterness, when it could be the most wonderful, peaceful and rewarding time of their lives.

A: What do we do about it?

J: It's pretty delicate to suggest that they might be one-upping and put-downing.

A: Even though it's so apparent.

J: Yes. I used to recommend a technique that worked for a lot of couples, those who recognized and acknowledged that they had a problem.

A: What was that?

J: Are you ready for this? I suggested that if they are in the habit of saying their prayers at night, that they kneel across the bed from one another, and the wife ends her prayers by saying, aloud, how she feels about an issue which is troubling both of them. The other is not allowed to respond. They go to bed and spend the next day thinking about it. The next night, the husband gets to speak aloud, expressing how he feels about the issue, and she is not allowed to respond. The third night, they are allowed to exchange thoughts, still on their knees.

A: Wow. I like that. And I could do that. I still get on my knees at night, and they're arthritic.

J: Probably have lots to confess.

A: You got that right.

J: I think this would be a great message for young people.

The Message is not the Medium

A: Have you noticed how the greeting card business is changing? All these beautiful cards with thoughtful messages?

J: You mean the ones that say four ninety-five on the back?

A: Yeah, they're expensive, but when you get one of them in the mail, they make you feel good, like somebody really cared.

J: Not just a twenty-five center anybody could send.

A: Right, and they're available in different places now, not just card shops. They're in Whole Foods, coffee houses, wherever people with disposable income line up to pay the cashier.

J: I try to stay away from those places. I clip coupons for the bargain supermarkets.

A: Look. I received this card yesterday. I want you to read the message.

J: It says,   Free your heart from hatred. Forgive.

                  Free your mind from worries: most worries never happen.

                  Live simply and appreciate what you have.

                  Give more.

                  Expect less.

A: Nice reminders, right? Not just thinking of you.

J: If only it were that simple. Interesting that it starts with forgive. I think forgiving ourselves is often more difficult than forgiving someone else, someone who hurt us.

A: Yes, but the total message tells us how to live our lives.

J: That's really what we were trying to do at the Institute.

A: The Boston College years?

J: Right. Those were probably the best years, well, the most productive years, of my life. We were bringing together leaders from all different religions in week-long seminars, emphasizing the commonalities of our beliefs rather than the differences.

A: You were writing verses for Hallmark and you didn't know it.

J: You dare make light of one of my peaks of achievement?

A: You see me kneeling in reverence here. I'm making light, but I know you organized the whole thing, and that it made a difference in the lives of a whole lot of people for many years following.

J: Thank you. That's more like it. You know, it all started with my wonderful wife, Mary, who at that time was Mother

Mary Hanley and she ran the Cenacle Retreat House. She had planned a workshop for some two hundred Cenacle Sisters from all over the United States and had already lined up three noted speakers from New York, Chicago and Toronto. They were specialists in Scripture, Dogmatic and Moral Theology, and Current Literature in Religion. She wanted me to be the other speaker, I suppose, because of my psychological training, which was unusual for a Jesuit.

A: Maybe she had spies who told her that you were also a very good speaker, and teacher.

J: Well, maybe. Anyway, that workshop was the spark for the Institute, We ran three more summer workshops, and they led to making it permanent. I spent the last four years in the Jesuits helping it grow, and it's still going strong.

A: That's your legacy.

J: Yes.

Real world

A: Let's talk about the real world today.

J: Could we narrow that down a little?

A: I mean how it's presented, by the media, by the government, by the corporations, by Wall Street, by the Church, compared to the way it really is.

J: That's a delicious topic.

A: We like to think we're going to leave a better world to our kids and their kids, but in reality, they aren't going to like us very much.

J: You're right. The debt alone, the world debt, is staggering.

A: People like to say, "Oh, don't worry about it. Every generation, as the people get older, they say the same thing. They can't imagine how the new generation will survive."

J: You're going to say that this time it's different.

A: Well, this time the real world is moving at a pace no one could have imagined. The little kids in the next generation will probably make fun of the iPod and iPad.

J: Ancient technology. Antiques.

A: I wish there were enough brave souls who understood the new media and could find ways to get an honest message across. You know, gradually take over the media empire as we know it now: the likes of Murdoch, anything for a dollar. That would be a start.

J: You're going to say, "The media *is* big business."

A: You've been paying attention. Hey, there's an idea. I'll bring up a subject and you tell me what you think I would say about it.

J: OK. I should nail these.

A: How would I describe today's television?

J: A new array of good-looking women cheerfully assuring us that everything is great with America. No problems, just be happy, like us.

A: That was good. How would I describe Congress?

J: K Street is the strongest arm of government. Home of the lobbyists.

A: Right on.

J: A bunch of fat cats who long ago forgot all about what is right for the citizens and are concerned only about whether the Republicans or Democrats are going to get a bigger share of the pie.

A: Excellent. What about religion?

J: They all say, "Ours is the only way." They can't all be right.

A: You got that right. What about peace on earth?

J: Never happen. Never has happened. If we don't soon find a way, we're headed for nuclear Armageddon.

A: What do you think about the military-industrial complex?

J: I think it's alive and kicking but hidden mostly by the media's slogan, "support our brave troops." We should transfer a chunk of that money and put it in peaceful pursuits as an example to the rest of the world. You're an idealist.

A: How about Wall Street?

J: Greed. Personified. At its height. Unbelievable bonuses to the top thieves. A legalized Las Vegas where the house fixes the take and allows the peons to play with the toys. Or words to that effect. You really hate those guys.

A: And the banks?

J: Probably worse than Wall Street. White collar thieves willing to kite mortgages into the skies and stall foreclosures until they can take back the homes of people they've screwed. Only you'd probably say it more succinctly.

A: You're doing fine. What would I say about cancer research?

J: Mouse grants. That all the research money is poured into a bottomless pit. Small improvements in treatments rather than prevention. Nobody really wants to find a cure.

A: Is that all?

J: You'd probably say that it's a conspiracy. That all the companies who are profiting from cancer, the medical profession, all the people who are employed, constitute a gigantic cash cow that needs to be nourished.

A: What's wrong with that?

J: That cancer now hits one out of three men and one out of two women, or the other way around. Anyway, it's a crime. We accept the premise that cancer can't be cured.

A: Is anybody doing anything about it?

J: No. We only think so, because we are duped by the Race for the Cure propaganda that rallies the naïve public while the puppets in the National Cancer Institute and American Cancer Society snicker in their closets.

A: Now, you've got it. What would you say about the big pharmaceutical companies and their clinical trials?

J: That ethics have gone out the window. They think nothing of highlighting the one or two favorable things they can say and omitting the fact that a few people died while taking the medicine being tested.

A: And the nation's health program?

J: It will be a miracle if they can ever come up with a plan. This Congress? Are you kidding me?

A: You get an A on your paper.

Laughing at our Limps and Lumps

A: Wasn't it Bette Davis who first said "old age ain't for sissies?"

J: Maybe. I think a lot of us would go along with that, but she and Spencer Tracy had long careers. I think they overcame some of the trials that catch up with all of us.

A: Like Mother Teresa. Buries her own problems by working with others.

J: That's probably the secret. We laugh at our infirmities. Getting in and out of the car is a good example. Somebody should video the two of us, you with your arthritic knees, me with my hip replacement that's out of joint.

A: My wife has had a hip, knee, shoulder, and now, an ankle replacement. She likes to say, "As long as they don't run out of spare parts, I'll be OK."

J: I think of Randy Pausch, the professor at Carnegie Mellon who wrote a book called, *"The Last Lecture,"* knowing that he was on the way out, with only a few short months to live with his cancer, and instead of holing up in hospice, he's out there giving talks, encouraging young people to discover their passion and live a full life.

A: I have the CD. He isn't saying live it up, have fun, make a lot of money so you can buy things.

J: No. He's saying "get involved, make a difference, make things better for others, wherever you go, whatever you do."

A: Strange how it takes a major setback for us to see the obvious.

J: Human nature, I guess. One of my best friends had polio, a priest like me, had polio and walked with a noticeable limp.

A: My first wife, the same.

J: He often said how others avoided him.

A: Yes, but when people do get to know them, they discover a spirit, a quality we don't have. An acceptance, maybe. They somehow rejoice in it.

J: That's him. They don't just overcome their handicap. They make a positive out of it.

A: We had a blind pastor give the sermon this morning. His wife went up the steps with him, and from that point on, you would never know that he couldn't see. His delivery, his whole relaxed manner reflected confidence, almost as if he was grateful for having been given a special gift.

J: That's a great way to put it. If only we could all do that.

A: One of our friends in our small group, Kim Kohegan, probably in her 50s, husband a doctor, ironically. She's suffering from a form of cancer, like my brother. At this stage, she gets terrible migraines, along with the treatments, that last for days. Yet, when you meet her, she's bright and lively, cheering *you* up. My brother, same way. For nine years now, the cancer has moved from one part of his body to another, they can't give him any more chemo or radiation. I'd be waiting for the shoe to drop. Yet, he is always cheerful, and productive! He writes columns for the major newspaper up in Maryland that reflect his positive attitude.

J: I had a patient who was bi-polar. Young lady, sixteen, who was putting her parents through a ringer, really wild and resentful, the whole magilla. I first met them when I was working on the high school principals' program, and they asked me if I would talk with her. What an experience.

A: You could write a book?

J: And then some. She was a one-woman wrecking crew.

A: Did you bring her around?

J: Yes. But the first couple of meetings were mostly listening, as you can imagine. I was able to get through to her, mostly with humor. I taught her how to laugh at situations, and laugh at herself. Now she gives me more credit than I deserve.

A: You still work with her?

J: No, but we have kept in touch for many years. All during her college years, we emailed one another.

A: Part of your "family" out there.

J: Yes.

A: Laughter helped me a lot with one of the men I was assigned to in the caregiving program. He had gone through colon cancer three years previously, all through the 16 chemo treatments, and he had returned to near normal. Then, after three years, it suddenly recurred. He was in his second week of the second round of chemo when we first got together, and he was not a happy puppy. He knew his days were numbered, and the best he could hope for wasn't good.

J: Familiar story.

A: We'd meet for coffee at Hardee's, he loved their cinnamon buns, two for a buck, and after a couple of weeks, I got him to open up on his Army days. He had been in the Battle of the Bulge in WWII, wounded. I was a year younger. By the time I got over there, the war had ended, but we traded stories about our Army days, and that got us into other stories about our early days, our girlfriends and other embarrassments, and we found a lot to laugh about.

J: Did he make it? Recover?

A: No, but he made it interesting. After his 16th chemo, he was feeling really good, and he and his wife took off for a visit to old friends in their home town in the Blue Ridge mountains, about a four-hour drive. They stayed at a bed and breakfast overlooking a small lake, having a great time, and the next night they met three other couples at a little restaurant back in the hills. They all said goodbye in the parking lot, and as Frank and his wife walked to their car, his insides imploded. She managed to get him in the car, but in her panic, she turned left instead of right and drove for 15 minutes in the wrong direction. It's nine o'clock at night, pitch dark, unfamiliar country road. She finally makes it back to the Bed and Breakfast, Frank moaning all the way, wakes the proprietor who calls her son who lives five miles away, and he leads them to the nearest hospital in Asheville, where the resident in ER informs her that they do not have the facilities to take care of Frank. So they load him in the ambulance for the four-hour ride back here. I get the call at five in the morning, His wife meets me at the front entrance and leans on me in our walk back to intensive care. We open the door. It's almost surreal. There's this body lying there, tubes draining fluids out, tubes pouring IVs and medications in. I leaned over him to say goodbye, and said, "Frank . . ." With that, his eyes opened, a faint smile, and he said, "Did you bring the coffee?"

J: Wow. What a story. He was having fun right up till the very end.

A: Yes, those were his last words.

Manufacturing Stress

A: You've mentioned a couple of times that you made a living talking to executives about stress.

J: That's a fact. I traveled all over the world delivering talks at these big conferences held for CEOs and top executives of major corporations.

A: Did you give them a stress test?

J: No, not intentionally, anyway. No, I had a basic message built around laughter, fantasy and art.

A: Fantasy and art? For executives?

J: Well, I admit, it was mostly laughter. I worked in a lot of funny stuff, jokes, situations, humorous take-offs on some of the famous philosophers.

A: Like Mark Twain.

J: Yes, absolutely. He got a lot of play. Along with Will Rogers. But I could take them back to Socrates. Laughter goes way back.

A: Right, I'll bet even the Apostles had a good time, maybe sometimes when Jesus wasn't around. Do you think they told jokes when they were out in the boat?

J: We'll never know, but you're probably right.

A: Maybe about their exploits with women, just like today.

J: More likely, their failures. Women didn't get their due throughout history. But no, I'd tell them the story about Norman Cousins.

A: What was that?

J: At one point, Cousins became very ill, and the doctors ran out of treatments. They gave him only a few months to live. They set him up with a wing in the hospital where he could slowly expire with as little pain and discomfort as possible.

A: Like hospice today.

J: Right. But Cousins had another idea. He talked his doctor into letting him stay in a hotel room where he could watch all the old classics, like the Honeymooners, Laurel and Hardy, the old silents, all the funny stuff, a steady diet of laughter.

J: Charlie Chaplin, Benny Hill, Jack Benny?

A: Fred Allen, Bob Hope, Bob Newhart . . .

J: Rodney Dangerfield, he's outrageous . . .

A: And Don Rickles, insulting everybody . . .

J: Sid Caesar, Carl Reiner . . .

A: Woody Allen, George Carlin . . .

J: Henny Youngman. We could go on forever, but that's the kind of stuff Cousins was watching.

A: Art Carney discovering Alice's new recipe for chicken salad in Gleason's ice box.

J: And they come up with a national campaign to introduce this incredible new taste to America, only to discover that it was really dog food.

A: Laurel and Hardy, "Now, see what you've done."

J: You remember.

A: So what happened to Cousins?

J: After just two months of laughter, his symptoms disappeared, and he went back to normal.

A: That's incredible. That sounds like something you made up.

J: No, it's a fact. Laughter has enabled a lot of people to get through an illness.

A: Well, I have seen something like that happen with several close friends and family. My brother has been putting up with cancer for over nine years. One of my other brothers died of cancer at age 55, but they both found ways to laugh through the whole routine.

J: Carney and Gleason did a lot of fantasizing. That's another way. It was a whole new idea for executives, and when I'd first start suggesting it, I could see them kind of looking at each other out of the corners of their eyes. But once they got into it, they loved it. It released them from the reality and enabled them to open up their thinking, to a whole new realm of possibilities, things they never considered, because they were weighed down with real problems, affecting lots of people..

A: You did them a big favor. You really made a difference in their lives.

J: It was rewarding for me. I even got them to study the old masters and discover in their paintings and sculptures the stories behind each masterpiece, the lessons of life that these creative people were providing for the generations that followed.

A: Nouwen wrote an entire book on the painting of the Prodigal Son.

J: Great example. I even got them to think about how it would be for people they had to lay off. I'd take them through the steps of loss, you know, shock, anger, grief, acceptance, self worth down the tank.

A: Did they accept that? They weren't turned off?

J: Several would mention after a session that I had made them think about it, that there wasn't much they could do about it in the face of competition, especially global, and the fact that goods could be produced so cheaply in other countries.

A: I know. It's hard to sell the idea that companies have a responsibility to all the people, not just their employees, to citizens as well as shareholders.

J: If we were running a company, we would be forced to do the same thing. Send the jobs overseas.

A: I understand that. But there's a major upheaval taking place. Those fifteen million jobs are never coming back. Technology is moving so fast that if someone is unemployed for just a few months, he has fallen so far behind he will never catch up.

J: You've said before that companies will have to invest in new ventures.

A: Even then, the manufacturing part of the venture will go overseas, as well as a lot of the technical. Robots are already replacing humans, on a big scale. For years, our companies have taken advantage of low wages in third world countries. Now it's coming back to bite our tail.

J: You see a dark picture.

A: Yes. I think it's reality. I also think the media has some responsibility in this, along with today's social networks, right down to the hand-helds. The message is that everything's going to be OK, just keep spending whatever money you have, or can borrow.

J: Which brings us back to the individual.

A: And stress. There would be a hell of a lot more stress if people understood what is happening.

J: I think we, individuals, have to find our inner strengths, our search for the soul, our purpose in life, the meaning of life to each of us, to discover and define our own value system.

A: That's a big order. We're going to meditate? Take up Yoga?

J: If that's our cup of tea. We have to open up our thinking. Get the negatives out of the way.

A: Define our brand, who do we want to be?

J: Yes. How do we want to live the rest of our lives? What do we want to accomplish? We have to recapture our self worth, become aware that there is only one of us in the entire world with our set of genes and the specific conditioning of those genes.

A: And we have to keep our sense of humor.

J: Living life is no picnic.

The Malaise of the Unemployed

A: You know, there's this strange malaise laying over the country, like a blanket, that says, "Well, there's nothing we can do about it, anyway, so why get all worked up about it?"

J: You think so?

A: I see it in working with the unemployed. Here we are with at least fifteen million people out of work, their jobs are not coming back, the jobs are over in Asia, or they've been eliminated by technology, yet most of the unemployed will not do the homework necessary to locate a job in the new marketplace.

J: Why is that?

A: You tell me. I work with church groups and groups at the community college. Ten to twenty people show up the first night. I describe the realities of the economy, of the new workplace, I get them together in groups of four to five, to do the researching, the homework, and be accountable to one another.

J: So what happens?

A: Six or seven will show up the next week. Maybe three have Googled some background on a company. Two or three will probably show up for a couple more weeks and maybe work at it enough to end up with a foot in the door at a growth company.

J: The rest do what?

A: Squat. That's what I mean by malaise. They're waiting for something to happen. They go to networking meetings at the churches where they can console each other. They hear that ABC company is hiring, so they dutifully send their resumes and tell themselves, and their wives, that they are doing a job search.

J: That's the way it used to be? Is that what you're saying?

A: Yes. They're discouraged. You can imagine. Most of them had pretty good jobs with big companies. Security. benefits. Then suddenly they're on the street. They never really had to work hard to find a job. Something would turn up, because the economy was healthy. But today? No way. Some of them have been out of work for fourteen months. They've settled in on unemployment checks, the wife is working, he's Mister Mom with the kids, they're somehow adjusting, but foreclosure is just around the corner. They've given up. If they do show up at one of my classes, they're ready to dispute any positive suggestion with their particular tale of woe, they're seeking solace from the rest of the group, some of whom are nodding their heads in agreement.

J: Woooeee. It's that bad?

A: I'm not exaggerating.

J: What are you trying to get them to do?

A: Two basic things. Really, one. Study today's job marketplace, and that will reveal two opportunities. The existing opportunity is in the health field, for obvious reasons. The population is getting older. Old people make up an increasing market for products and services. Something like seventy six million Boomers will turn 65 in a few months.

J: Some hope there?

A: The future opportunities are in the emerging markets, like energy, green, sustainable buildings, the infrastructure, high tech, of course. So their assignment is to redirect their work experience into the existing companies and into the new and different companies. Growth companies in growth fields.

J: So will they have to add new skills?

A: More than likely. They will have to really study the new market to find a niche, to determine what they can bring to a start-up or a company on the way up.

J: I'm sitting here thinking what would I be doing.

A: Well, you'd have far less of a problem because of your doctorate in clinical psychology. That kind of sets you up for some special, and unusual, opportunities.

J: I went to prison.

A: Yeah, but in the front door.

J: How do you see the job market improving?

A: Only as the economy improves. Consumers are not spending enough money to spur the economy, and won't be until the unemployed start earning real incomes. They can't do that until the companies start investing the profits they're sitting on into areas that promise growth, and they won't do that until they're practically guaranteed more profits.

J: We're at a standstill.

A: Right. We can't depend on the fat cats , the wealthy one percent, to spend enough to spur the economy. They spend less, relatively, than we do. They put their money into more investments so they can spread the gap between the one percent and the rest of us.

J: I understand that. I read where the top one percent thirty years ago took in about nine per cent of the country's total income compared to now when they take in something like twenty-three percent.

A: And we can't look to the government to come up with real solutions. People today, especially the Rush Limbaughs and Glenn Becks and Sarah Palins, demean the stimulus plans. Certainly they weren't big enough, but the real problem is that they weren't used for the purpose they were intended. Here in North Carolina, four hundred million dollars in stimulus money which was earmarked for creating new jobs was used to pay off part of the previous year's debt. Not a penny for new jobs.

J: What's the solution?

A: To get people back to work, for one. Obama's trusted financial experts got us involved instead in saving the big banks so that they could continue to pay themselves big bonuses. One day historians will look back on these times and say no wonder a guy like Madoff got away with his Ponzi scheme. Wall Street has pulled the wool over the eyes of Washington for years.

J: I feel another tirade coming on.

A: I'll go easy on them this time. Let me just suggest that Wall Street should be regarded as a giant Las Vegas casino. The House fixes the bets and calls the shots. Investors gamble, they bet on how other people will bet, on how fast those other people will gain or lose, and the House and Wall

Street banks, gets a piece of all the action. They're called bonuses. Nobody on Wall Street produces anything. Wall Street doesn't contribute anything to the economy. There's no product. There's no service, except to provide the numbers to the bettors. They just post the odds during the wee hours so that day traders can have some fun before the common gamblers wake up. Soon they won't even have to do that. The bettors will have all the odds on their wrist watch.

J: I'm glad you went easy on them.

A: Some day I'll take off on K Street in Washington. There's some real money changing hands there, and there's no risk involved. It's an entrenched system that the Brotherhood keeps sacred. K Street is now our strongest branch of government.

J: Whoooeee. You're on a roll.

A: All part of the malaise. There's nothing we can do about it, so why worry about it?

J: In all honesty, what do you think we can do about it?

A: I'd like to think that an informed public would be so incensed that they would rise up in force, start facing up to our problems and start demanding real action.

J: That sounds a lot like the Tea Party.

A: Yes, unfortunately. Some of the noise they started with was well intentioned, but they allowed themselves to be taken over by Murdoch's Machine and his greedy group of pawns and opportunists, Limbaugh, Beck, Palin and the like. What we need is a legitimate national movement like the old NRA and WPA which shook us out of the Depression back in the thirty's. The National Recovery Act and the Works Projects Administration.

J: You and I remember the billboards along the roads with the big red-white-and-blue NRA logo.

A: My father and I painted many of them. He would outline the letters, and I would shuffle along next to him on the plank, filling them in. Everybody was working together back in those days to make things better for everybody.

J: Then World War Two really united us.

A: We learned as kids that we could do something about our problems. The war brought it home. Everyone was involved. All the sons were drafted or volunteered. All the parents went to work in defense plants. Today we send our reservists over, continually, to fight unwinnable wars that accomplish nothing.

J: Maybe we can devote some creative thinking as to how we can shake up the populace.

Cancer is Big Business

A: I was going through some old stuff and found an article in the Atlantic that set me off again.

J: Oh-oh.

A: Yeah, on that old theme of why our vaunted medical research can't come up with cures for cancer.

J: What did you find out?

A: Same old, same old, that the focus is always on a tangent, a so-called improvement of some other company's product already on the market. Nobody is really working on a cure.

J: Nobody?

A: Tell me who. If some lonely researcher were to come up with a real breakthrough, he would be gobbled up by a big company who would buy his approach and put it in the closet.

J: You said before that they would put him on their quack list.

A: Well, that's what the American Cancer Society would do, and probably the National Cancer Institute. Have you been to Washington and viewed the size of the NCI headquarters? A huge city block, four or five stories tall, What goes on in there?

J: Paper shuffling?

A: Exactly, only the shuffling today is all on the computers.

J: There must be some progress being made.

A: Show me where. Why isn't there some accounting? Some accountability? Why hasn't the Government, our watchdog Congress, all on the take, why hasn't someone said, "Show me the results of your research. Show me where the research grants have gone and what the results were. Do you mean to tell me that after 75 years of searching for a cure, the best you can come up with is chemotherapy and radiation? That's a solution? Killing a bunch of cells, hoping that you don't kill too many of the good cells in the process, and destroying the immune system altogether? That's the best you can do? You're drawing your paychecks every two weeks, your companies making the products are making big profits. Looking for a cure? Are you kidding me? Your R&D is simply trying to improve your competitions' improvement. That's the best you can do? After 75 years?"

J: You're really wound up.

A: We'd better get wound up. As a nation. How many people do you know who have cancer or have died of cancer? Three out of ten families experience cancer, maybe more today. Two of my brothers, one gone, one still fighting for his life. He has been through so many rounds of chemo and so many treatments of radiation that they cannot give him any more. Cancer keeps moving from one area in his body to another.

J: It's an awful illness.

A: I've been assigned to three men, watching them die of cancer, two with colon cancer, both with months of suffering, another with bone marrow transplants that didn't take. He died on a grotesque stem cell machine, did you ever see one, that looked like something out of a torture chamber, shaking this hulk of a man like a rag doll.

J: What can we do about it?

A: That's just the point. Like so many other issues, we feel like there's nothing we can do about it. We're lulled into this apathy, numbed would be a better word, by the media machine that keeps us entertained and out in left field. There is no principle other than making money. Say anything. Keep the pot boiling. Run more ads, "We support Race for the Cure."

J: We've been down this road.

A: I know. I sound like a broken record. This latest article sets me off. It demonstrates, it documents, the fact that medical research is, in their words, pervasively flawed, that most of the studies start with a goal to be supported, that the results are tweaked to back up that goal, that a placebo is often as effective as the three medications being tested, but even a fledgling copywriter can find a hook to feature.

J: I've read about studies being irresponsible, and often shaded by conflicts of interest.

A: Doctors on the take, doctors owning three and four big clinics, buying and selling chemotherapy. Do they want to see a cure?

J: We see all the politicians criticizing the health plan. At least it's a start.

A: It's a joke. It's an easy avenue for politicians to gain some votes. Somehow we have to wake up, shake up, and just plain explain to people what is happening to America.

J: Nobody's laughing, except maybe the people on Wall Street.

A: We should talk some more about this.

Peace will have to wait

J: Last week you asked about world peace.

A: Another minor problem.

J: And we took off on violence. I meant to mention that for a short time, Mary and I were active in the Fellowship for Reconciliation.

A: Sounds religious.

J: It *is* an interfaith organization, embracing all religions or no religions, that seeks to replace violence, war, racism and economic injustice with nonviolence, peace and justice.

A: That's a tall order.

J: It's a commitment to active nonviolence as a transforming way of life and as a means of radical change.

A: How do you carry out a mission like that?

J: By example, like we said last week. In our daily lives, in our daily communication with others. Your son-in-law believes that peace isn't possible, and that the alternative is unavoidable. Extinction. I may be a dreamer, but I'd like to think the Lord had other things in mind.

A: I'm sure you're right, but maybe the cards are stacked against us.

J: I think he expects us to not just wave the banner, but take an active part in fostering peace in our daily lives. Granted, it's an uphill battle.

A: Really. It's one of those huge intangibles. People figure they can't do anything about it, anyway, so why think about it.

J: We have to think about it. The way we're headed, conducting wars to foster peace is insane.

A: Eisenhower saw it coming. He warned us about the military-industrial complex, a permanent military machine that would dominate our actions and threaten our livelihood, and here we are, trying to be the world's police force.

J: Ike helped us avoid a nuclear war, because we were in control. Not now. I remember reading that when he joined the Army, it numbered 84,000, but during his time in office, it had grown to 840,000. No telling what it is today.

A: I was going to use the word entrenched, no pun intended, to describe that our problems are entrenched in Washington. Do you think it's possible to rally enough people to bring about change?

J: Not the way we are regarded today. We are consumers, not citizens. Our media, you've pointed out, could be providing the rallying force we need, but they are also the entrenched, just like all the other big corporations sitting on their money.

A: They won't be spending any of it to bring about change. That's a scary word for those sitting pretty.

J: Like that quote, "a desk is a scary place from which to view the world." Something like that. But I don't know how we'd ever get a rallying force together.

A: Maybe if things get bad enough, or *when* they get bad enough, the unemployed will rise up. Right now, and for some time to come, they're drawing their weekly stipend and quietly adjusting.

J: It would take a Congress made up of one-term, dedicated people working for the good of everybody else.

A: Like the founding fathers intended.

J: It will never happen.

A: Not in our lifetime, that's for sure. But what will the world be like for our grandchildren?

Peace in our day?

A: Do you think peace in the world is a reachable goal? Realistically?

J: No, evidently not, but I think we have to keep trying.

A: Man has been at war from the earliest times. Do you think the Creator anticipated that? Or do you think he, or she, hoped that man could live peacefully?

J: The latter.

A: What if there were other earths in the galaxy with human beings constantly at wars, various kinds of wars, and we're all in some kind of competition to see which ones last the longest. Maybe we're all headed for Armageddons and when one completely annihilates itself, another is begun.

J: That's a sorry outlook, but we will never know.

A: I have a son-in-law, a brilliant surgeon who reads the Bible every morning. He says peace in the world was never a goal, that wars are inevitable, and that God says that it is perfectly all right for one nation to wipe out evil in another nation. In fact, he gave the early generals permission and even told them how to go about it.

J: Well, I know that "it is written . . . ," but I agree that man has not given peace a chance down through the centuries. We have now reached a point where Armageddon is a reality. We have weapons that can wipe out civilizations. Hitler and the Nazis developed the atomic bomb, and we've enhanced it ever since.

A: How do we counter that kind of might? In the hands of Iran and North Korea and Libya and probably a half dozen others we don't know about.

J: Maybe there is hope, if enough people, and nations, show by example that world peace is a viable goal. Thomas Merton had a short piece on enemies. Hang on a minute. I may have it right here, somewhere. Here it is. He says, "Do not be too quick to assume that your enemy is also an enemy of God just because he is your enemy. Perhaps he is your enemy precisely because he can find nothing in you that offers glory to God." In other words, we could start by working on the violence in our hearts.

A: Yes, *individuals* assassinated JFK and Bobby Kennedy and Martin Luther King.

J: Violence is everywhere, in every country, in every citizen. We think of it only in places like the military, or the Mafia, criminals. But it's in our entertainment on television, the fake wrestling productions, now the caged fighters inflicting punishment that take us back to the Romans turning loose the lions on the inmates for the delight of the good citizens.

A: And in our computer games and movies for television.

J: Everywhere. In our churches! Our schools, hospitals, prisons, think about it, in our own homes, our neighborhoods, sports, banks – yes, banks, you think they haven't been violent?

A: All different kinds of violence.

J: In *us* as well. When someone cuts us off on the road, what's our reaction? We want to speed up and cut them off. Get even.

A: Violence in the home the same way. Husbands and wives putting each other down incessantly until one, or both, explodes.

J: Exactly. Get this: Ted Nugent, a spokesman for the NRA, spoke recently to 20,000 cheering fans at the convention center. His talk was titled *Mother Theresa with a Glock,* and he promoted three things: one, pass a law for hunting on Sunday; two, join the NRA; and three, get your kid's Principal to allow you to bring an M16 into the school to show kids how to use it.

A: Wow. And we'd be saying give peace a chance. I shouldn't be surprised. My own neighbor, a big, burly guy, confided that he now carries the smallest .45 available in a holster underneath his armpit.

J: Nugent finished by saying, "Kids, you say that war is not the answer. That is what Ozzy Osbourne says, and he's retarded."

A: And that says it all.

What for the Metaphor?

A: Did you use a lot of metaphors and analogies in your talks?

J: Did I ever.

A: The audience remembers the metaphors, right?

J: Right. The metaphors connect with something they already accept with a better way to remember it. You have given them something valuable, memorable they can add to their arsenal. They're grateful, and you have earned their respect.

A: Quotations, the same way.

J: You bet. We don't have to be brilliant, just quote brilliant people.

A: They've already done the thinking.

J: When we know or can sense how our audience feels, then we can connect our feelings to theirs and theirs to ours.

A: I tried to get that point across in my workshops: it all starts with the audience. Their point of view. I'd try to tell those CEOs that it's not about them. I'd tell them that whenever someone asked them to be a speaker, they should ask for an audience breakdown, to determine where they are coming from, their attitudes, their hot buttons.

J: That's so basic, but so many times speakers ignore it and then wonder why they laid an egg.

A: I had one guy who learned that lesson. He was delivering his standard speech for doctors when he suddenly realized he was talking to nurses, some of them male.

J: It's the audience's point of view that matters; then in our planning, we know which quotes to feature, which analogies. Later, when we deliver them and see all the heads nodding agreement, it's a wonderful feeling. We've got 'em in the palm of our hand.

A: We quote Socrates and the audience puts us right up there with all the learned.

J: Learned. "Knowing things makes you learned; knowing yourself makes you wise." That's a quote I used a lot. We could be accused of manipulating the minds of those in the audience, using a technique to reinforce our own convictions and plant them on the unwary.

A: As in religion.

J: There you go again. But yes, people who know how the mind works, its insulas and cingulated cortices, ahem, I threw that in there to impress you, can use it to promote good, or evil.

A: Religions have used metaphors for ages; the scribes probably threw in a couple of insulated cornices of their own.

J: Probably.

A: Bread and wine for body and blood.

J: Perfect. Association is a strong technique. Especially with the emotions.

A: Body and blood gives me an immediate picture of Christ on the cross; bread and wine, the Last Supper.

J: Body and Blood says Communion to me, and you can't go to Communion unless you've gone to Confession. Now, for your penance say five Our Father's and Five Hail Mary's, and stop picking on religions, and come back here next week with five metaphors that stir positive emotions.

A: That's a deal, and we can talk about our favorite quotations at the same time.

J: I came across a great quote just this morning. Listen to this:

> The budget should be balanced, the Treasury should be refilled,
>
> public debt should be reduced, the arrogance of officialdom should be
>
> tempered and controlled, and the assistance to foreign lands should
>
> be curtailed lest Rome become bankrupt. People must again learn to
>
> work, instead of living on public assistance.

A: Rome? Who said that?

J: Cicero. Cicero in the year 55 b.c.

A: You're kidding. Read it again.

J: "The budget should be balanced, the Treasury should be refilled, public debt should be reduced, the arrogance of officialdom should be tempered and controlled, and the assistance to foreign lands should be curtailed lest Rome become bankrupt. People must again learn to work, instead of living on public assistance."

A: It fits today. Partly.

J: Some things change, and some things never change.

Propheteering and God's Word

A: The pastor's Christmas message was a Bible lesson attesting to the absolute fact that Jesus was the answer to all the prophecies exhorted by some 300 prophets, and of course, he was in the direct lineage of King David, because his earthly father Joseph was a second cousin of Herod's mistress.

J: I never knew that.

A: It's true. It said so right there in the 4-color brochure they distributed with the second collection.

J: Where do I begin here? Let's start with the prophets.

A: OK, the pastor said there were 300 prophets heralding the coming of the Messiah. Of course none referred to the Messiah as Jesus. They referred to a king who would appear out of nowhere and right the wrongs of the world, as they knew it.

J: They weren't looking for the Baby Jesus.

A: Who disappeared for 30 years, incidentally, except for a visit to the Temple when he was twelve years old and got shooed out the side door for his audacity.

J: Well, it was generally accepted that a great prophet would appear, yes.

A: It was also generally accepted that the world would come to an end, the Perousia, before the next generation would see the light of day.

J: You want me to defend the Old Testament?

A: No, but it was painful to hear him move from one prophet to another, citing one premise to back up another premise. What for? Brainwashing, that's all it is. People quote the Old Testament as if it's fact. That makes me angry.

J: Catholics got smart a long time ago, calling them Gospels and concentrating on Matthew, Mark, Luke and John. Not Gospel truths, necessarily, but your point is made. We do quote the Bible and Gospels as God's word.

A: Exactly. It's *man's* word. Man's word about God. It's dishonest to refer to them as God's word. And *presumptuous?!* We're going to have some tall explaining to do when we arrive at the pearly gates.

J: You're getting worked up again.

A: Matthew and Luke couldn't even agree on Christ's birth. Matthew has three kings traveling three thousand miles, prodding their donkeys to hurry up before somebody pulls the plug on that giant light in the sky. Luke gets it right with shepherds tracking sheep dung into the stable.

J: Such irreverence. It's easy to refute the scriptures.

A: Even the word "scriptures" has gained a hallowed connotation, as if they are above questioning. Why not be honest and call them stories or anecdotes or exaggerations passed along by people of the times, some of whom were probably intelligent and some of whom may have had their own agendas or were paid to say different things by the king or some group of lobbyists.

J: Would you say there's some truth mixed in there somewhere?

A: Sure. A lot of the stories may have been based on something that might have happened.

J: I like to think that most of the writers were trying to record what was happening.

A: But they were recording their interpretations and exaggerations along with it, trying to reach the people of their times. Why do we now, in this day and age, feel compelled to accept the wild exaggerations as facts? Jonah in the Whale, Noah and the Ark? Do we like brainwashing our little kids?

J: You think it's brainwashing. Maybe they're just metaphors gone wild.

A: Give me a break. Walk into any church pre-school and see the big colorful cut-outs of the Ark and the Whale on the walls, down the halls. The kids are told that Jonah lived inside the whale for three days! What's the purpose?

J: I've heard this before. Then when the kids get a little older, they stop believing in Santa Claus.

A: Exactly. Why not stick to the truth. If it's a story, tell us it's a story. If there's a lesson in the story, bring the lesson up to date, we'll get it.

J: You get pretty worked up about all this.

A: Absolutely. Tough enough to raise kids today. Starting them out on nonsense is unforgivable.

The Rise of the Unemployed

J: What we've talked about before has bothered me ever since. All that unemployment, and how difficult it is for people to get back to work.

A: You just said it. One of the problems is that we all think of it as "getting back to work," as in getting our old job back. Our old job is gone forever. We have no choice but to create our new job in a growth company.

J: When you express that in your workshops, do they get it? Are they doing the homework?

A: Very few. What's your guess? It's maybe one out of thirty, at best, will really follow through. Three or four more may get their feet wet. The great majority are caught up in the great malaise.

J: Is it really that bad?

A: I'm working with people who show up regularly at big church networking meetings every week, some in crowds of 400, even five hundred, but only a small minority are resourceful enough or assertive enough to do the research, to make good use of LinkedIn, for example. Persuading them to study companies in a field they are not familiar with is like pulling teeth.

J: What's the solution?

A: I wish I knew. I think the next few years are going to see a flood of homes going on the market, foreclosures, a lot of broken homes, broken marriages, broken families.

J: Unemployment is another product of our times, isn't it? A combination of an inept, if not corrupt, Congress, an escalation of greed like we have never seen before, corporations sitting on their profits, like you say, because they are beholden only to their shareholders.

A: Never mind all the people they have put on the street.

J: And a pandering media that keeps the populace entertained instead of informed. We've covered this ground before.

A: But that's where we are. I'm afraid it's going to take hitting bottom for Americans to wake up to the reality. The most important branch of government is on K Street, the lobbyists. What we need instead is a legitimate rallying force, not a Tea Party sponsored by the likes of a Rupert Murdoch, but one somehow rallying the fifteen million, and counting, unemployed people, getting them to rise up and inundate our representatives in Washington with the reminder that their days are numbered.

J: Wouldn't that be something! They get one term in office, that's it, like the founding fathers intended in the first place.

A: We've come so far away from being a united states. The last time we were united was during World War Two. But we have the numbers right now that could make a difference in the way the country is run and in the way corporations avoid responsibility to the people, not just their employees.

J: That's an interesting thought, but you'd have to legislate it, and it would never happen.

A: Probably. The media would be the last to go after big business, because they are big business. Maybe a dozen companies own the world's media. They followed Sarah Palin around like a puppy dog, because they knew advertisers would settle for a small percentage of people they can count on to buy their products.

J: You're on a roll here.

A: I know I'm dreaming, but wouldn't it be great if we could mobilize the unemployed? Fifteen million votes, and counting, plus all the college graduates and near-graduates who will be living back home with their parents, because they couldn't find jobs. The few who do find work will be "interns," privileged to work for peanuts within the grand corporate structure. Management has discovered how easy it is to replace an older employee, along with his higher salary, perks and possible medical problems.

J: Are you being a little rough on the corporate world?

A: Not really. The media plays up Ford Motor paying back its loan. With government money! And what did they do with it? Built a giant facility in Brazil with five robotized assembly lines producing five different vehicles at once and providing thousands of jobs, for Brazilians!

J: They would answer that by saying, "You would do the same thing if you were running the company."

A: Yes, because then I would be answering only to the shareholders, not the citizens of my country. Ford could have built that same facility here in the states and put a lot of people to work. Of course, the shareholders would get a smaller dividend. Whatever happened to corporate responsibility?

J: It got shifted to the taxpayers. Us.

A: There was a time when companies cared about people, customers as well as employees. Heinz is a classic example. Years ago, they started treating employees as real people and their empire spread all over the world. Today customers are just consumers, and employees are just expendables.

J: The theme today is that the unions have caused all our problems by raising the standard of living for the workers.

A: What a crock.

J: Of course, cars can be produced for less in third world companies, because their wages are about one tenth of ours.

A: We can't compete, so we send the jobs over there. We now have a global workplace.

J: With a big void here at home.

Do you want God to find you a job?

A: Last week we started by talking about the economy.

J: Which led to God and the world.

A: So let's go back to your pretending to be one of the 15,000,000 unemployed.

J: I remember a period like that, vividly.

A: Me, too. Unemployment was a way of life for me. I free-lanced in New York for more than twenty years, and I was always looking for my next assignment. Anyway, back to our story: here you are, out of work. Where is God in your plans?

J: Hearing my prayer, I hope, to get back to work.

A: OK, let's say you hear that XYZ Company is hiring.

J: I send my resume?

A: Sit down a minute, you're in the Dark Ages. Put your resume away; it's probably too general anyway. It doesn't matter who is hiring unless you have the specific skills the company is looking for. So your first assignment you've already covered – asking the Lord for the patience and strength required to get through a tough job search. Now, you have to determine who you are, not a handsome dog who can do anything, but the sum total of your achievements from your career and personal life.

J: My personal life?

A: Yes. Where you have overcome hardship, made all-state as a running back, led the girls' choir, all that kind of thing.

J: On the resume?

A: *Within* the resume. You reflect some of them by changing all your job descriptions to achievement statements. Instead of, "I supervised a staff of nine, etc." you say, "I brought together two marketing departments to effect a saving of two hundred thousand dollars over a two-year period while increasing sales by 12%."

J: I get the idea.

A: You have to study the new workplace, the emerging markets. That's where patience comes in. You will probably find that you have to take on new skills that apply to areas like energy, infrastructure, speed rail and the like, and you are going to spend a lot of time on the internet and in visits to the local library.

J: I'm not good at that.

A: That's what they all say. Nine out of ten of the unemployed are caught up in a malaise of frustration and resentment. You are pretending here, but just imagine how you would feel if you had reached a comfort level in your previous job, with a good salary, perks, and especially, stature. You were respected, you had a position, maybe even a VP after your name. You feel entitled to more of the same.

J: That's all gone.

A: Now you have to stand in line at the unemployment office, and you see yourself in all the faces of a thousand others in the same boat.

J: I'd be praying.

A: Right. Which brings us back to, "Where is God in all this?"

J: You tricked me.

A: Maybe. Are you praying for God to give you a job? That's not his job, and resenting him for not giving you one is not a good way to land a permanent job in his company, if you get what I mean.

J: I get it. But is that what they do? Resent the Lord?

A: Most men do. They might say they resent their fate, but a good many live in that daydream of "if I live a good life," which translates to going to church on Sunday or reading the Bible, "then I have a right to expect that I will be rewarded."

J: That sounds familiar.

A: They have a tough time accepting the fact that their former job is not coming back, that it has been eliminated, either by technology, or it's now over in East Asia. They like to think that the economy will come back, like some giant balloon that has drifted off and will find its way back. They do not accept the need for studying some new field or some kind of start-up, and they're certainly not going to consider moving away, or selling the house and taking a loss. No way. They're adamant about refusing any kind of change.

J: Most of them?

A: Right. Typical. Meanwhile, the wife may be working, if he's lucky, and he may be one of the few who finds a part-time job stocking grocery shelves at night, or more than likely, just trying to adjust to living on the unemployment check and putting up with conditions that threaten the relationship, theirs and the kids.

J: Let me guess. My self worth is at a low level, my wife and kids treat me differently, I can't seem to do anything right, I hate taking out the garbage, going to church doesn't make me feel any better, and I'm beginning to resent the Lord for letting all this happen to me.

A: Exactly.

J: So what's the answer?

A: You have to augment the prayer with the hard work involved in creating your job in the emerging marketplace, or in the one existing marketplace, the health field.

J: The Lord will provide the strength and patience I need, maybe even some wisdom I didn't know I had, but I have to absorb my loss and get on with my life.

A: Then, you gather your list of achievements, study the growth companies in the new fields and come to grips with fact that you have to transfer your skills, and add new skills. Then you have to network like mad into those new companies, or into the old companies that are going in the new directions, like GE for example.

J: Sounds like a lot of work.

A: It sure is, but it's the only way. Unless your uncle happens to run one of those companies.

A personal relationship with God

A: I wonder if we could spend a little more time on one of the antidotes to religion that comes to the forefront as we get older.

J: I'm game.

A: I have a brother who, oddly enough, is about the same age as we are.

J: Ancient.

A: A couple of years older, so right between you and me.

J: Old, anyway.

A: Only now, after all these years, we find ourselves ready to talk about an evasive but strongly desired goal – a personal relationship with our maker.

J: Oh, that is a topic.

A: You know, I start each day saying hello to Jesus, the sculptured bust I made of him that sits there staring at me while I'm on the PC.

J: I do the same with the one you made for me.

A: But at the same time, I can't even presume for a minute that the God of all creation would spend so much as a second acknowledging my existence. How could God keep track of all his children, millions of them, all wanting his attention?

J: Usually wanting some *thing*. Most of our prayers are requests for something we need, or think we need, down here.

A: Yes. Which brings me to my brother. I had three older brothers, one died of cancer at 55, another is 95 in a retirement home up at the Cape. But the one I want to feature today has suffered from prostate cancer and its multitude of effects for almost ten years. Meanwhile, he goes through an almost endless series of chemo and radiation treatments. I say almost, because he has reached the point where they can't give him anymore.

J: Ouch.

A: They have him on some experimental routine, and he's hanging in there. Which is what he has done all through this. He's a good writer. He was a columnist for a major newspaper up in Maryland, writing on a wide range of topics in the public interest.

J: Good man.

A: Had a background in PR and worked for John Gardner at HEW in Washington.

J: John Gardner of Common Cause?

A: Right. And at HEW, the Department of Health, Education and Welfare, which you probably know. Anyway, he is well motivated, and has done a lot of good in his life.

J: I think you're about to say something like, we're praying for him, we're asking for something, in this case , for God to intercede down here.

A: You got it.

J: Do we dare pray for something specific? Will our prayers be answered?

A: Which prompts the same old answer: yes, our prayer will be answered, but in God's way and in God's time.

J: So, if that's the case, why do we pray?

A: Yes, do we pray because we want to believe that somehow, some way God will intercede?

J: I think so, yes. And we're not crazy. You and I have experienced some otherwise totally unexplainable occurrences. So have a lot of other people.

A: That's true. Many times I've said to myself, that's a God thing. An answered prayer.

J: So, can we conclude that God does answer our prayers?

A: Aye, there's the rub. Right back to sometimes, or all the times, but in his way and on his schedule.

J: We can be sure that the one who created all heaven and earth can make the right decision.

A: But sometimes it's very difficult to accept. I'm assigned to a young man right now whose brother was killed in an auto accident a short while ago. He asks, "Where is God in all this?"

J: Why do some people get cancer, like your brother, some get ALS, some get divorced?

A: Divorce is a good example of man creating his own problems, but let's stick for now with the happenings in our lives that seem to come out of nowhere. The ones that get most of our prayers.

J: That brings us back to your original premise. Do we have, or can we even presume to have a personal relationship with our Lord?

A: Right.

J: Well, we could define what we mean by relationship. Our friend Henri Nouwen in his writings says the good relationship is made up of two elements.

A: Respect and trust.

J: Right. Respect for one another and a trust in one another. Is it possible for us, two old and miniscule beings in a tiny spot on earth, to establish that with the God Almighty?

A: I hope so, but that's the question my brother and I have been kicking around on the email.

J: I don't think most of us would have a problem with respect, but I do think we choose many times to go our own way rather than trust in the Lord to make things right.

A: Amen to that. Yes, I think it's difficult for us to admit the fact that we put the Lord outside the door and expect him to be there when we're through having a good time.

J: Or just ignoring him most of the time. Like it's more important for us to get our work done or get the kids to soccer practice or just go shopping.

A: I wonder how many of the fifteen million people out of work have given up on the Lord.

J: Waiting for him to give them a job?

A: I know that many of them are praying for that. They gather at the big churches once a week for endless networking with one another, comforting each other, praying together.

J: Oh, and when they don't get a job, they get to feeling that the Lord isn't hearing them.

A: Right. There goes any chance of a personal connection. If the Lord can't find them a job, then why bother with all this resume writing and answering job postings?

J: That reminds me of that old saw about the missionary and the native who asks him, "If I hadn't learned all this about Jesus, would I still be able to get to Heaven?" The missionary thinks for a moment and says, "Well, yes." And the native says, "Then why did you tell me?"

A: Something like that. A lot of them have given up. Rather than scramble for the six-month assignment that will disappear to Indonesia or the meager part-time assignments that pay less than the unemployment check, they have settled for the unemployment check. When those run out, there's going to be hell to pay.

J: Money plays such an important part in our lives. We're going to see more broken homes, more marriages breaking up, more kids experiencing blended families.

A: Those will be the lucky ones. A good many will not be blended, and the kids are going to be very confused and resentful. Why is it so difficult for our so called leaders in Washington to see what is happening to the country? To millions of people. Families.

J: You've pointed out that Obama and his experts have diverted our attention to the deficit instead of creating jobs.

A: Because many of the people in Washington have no idea how to create jobs.

J: They attack the deficit, because that's easy, and they can pose as good stewards, making sure we don't go deeper into debt.

A: So there will be no way to support the areas that would produce jobs, the infrastructure for one.

J: That's the big picture. What we're talking about is the effect all this has on the individual. The guy who has been out of work for a year, or more, is surely having trouble finding God in all this. That personal connection has been torn apart.

A: Add to that all the people who are fighting a serious illness, like my brother and millions like him. People struggling with the problems us aging parents are presenting. Not just the cost, but the stress, the guilt involved in trying to show respect and at the same time put up with all the extra arrangements.

J: As a nation, we're in deep soup, as you say. As individuals, I wonder how we stack up when compared to our ancestors. Our parents lived through the Depression years. There were similar upheavals. Roosevelt was smart enough to establish the NRA and CCC and a bunch of other initials, but at one time, even he pulled out the rug from under the recovery and had to be coerced into putting the money back in.

A: They had a real deficit. It became obvious to them that they had to live with the deficit until the country recovered. We don't learn from history.

J: Back to the individual. As we get older, we feel the need to get closer to God. You and I are blessed, because we have experienced God in action. We have seen how he has appeared in our own lives and in the lives of others.

A: Yes. We know he's there for all of us. All we have to do is open the door.

J: Even in the toughest times.

A: Like now. We'll pray for patience and strength and wisdom.

J. He always answers that one.

The Throne

A: I was reading where most of the reading that most men do is on the throne.

J: Throne?

A: Toilet. Sitting on the can, reading.

J: Oh.

A: Some guy had done a study . . . now that would be interesting, how the hell would you do a study of guys sitting on the can reading . . . but anyway, he determined that for most men, that was the only place they did any reading at all.

J: Oh, that's a great commentary.

A: Think about it. I'll bet that's where you do some of your best thinking, as well as reading.

J: True. Except that a doctor once told me that that was a good way to get hemorrhoids, so I don't linger like I used to.

A: But I notice you've got a basket full of magazines right next to your commode.

J: Yes. Guilty. But I try not to spend too much time there.

A: Well, the average is 15 minutes. The average man spends 15 minutes on the can.

J: He doesn't want to hurry such a delicate operation.

A: I keep a basket full of old Harper's Indexes there. You know, all the crazy statistics. I have copies going back to 1985. It's fun to see what the nation was thinking about.

J: If it was anything like today, the nation wasn't thinking.

A: I'll bring some next week. Good for reflecting on signs of the times.

J: One reason I sit as long as I do is that it's so difficult for me to get back up.

A: Oh, me too. I keep wondering why most toilets are way down there. They get closer to the floor every year we get older.

J: You can buy higher ones today. And you can buy those seats that sit on top.

A: Of course, but then you have a longer flight down.

J: You're gross. But getting back up is a problem. My knees lock if I sit for very long.

A: Me, too. I have to rock back and forth for a few minutes, then propel myself forward, reaching for the sink, then pulling myself up.

J: I do that, too, keep telling myself, " nose over toes. nose over toes."

A : Really great, getting old. But in this study, imagine now. 2000 guys sitting on the can.

J: I'd rather not.

A: Well, imagine they aren't together in any one place, like in Symphony Hall or maybe the Vatican rotunda, and I have to question the veracity of the whole thing, but it's a great thought-starter.

J: I'll grant you that, but the whole thing stinks.

A: How come the bathroom has become the man's sanctuary? His safe-haven from the trials of the day.

J: The hiding place from his wife. She wouldn't dare come in there while he's working.

A: Wouldn't it be interesting to see what's in all those baskets next to the toilets, a real marker of man's intellectual aspirations.

J: No wonder the world's in peril.

A: The wife looks the other way, or the cleaning lady, if she spots a Playboy magazine. Let the old boy have some jollies with his imagination.

J: That's a sign of some marriages, a kind of resignation, that the physical act, sex, has pretty much been set aside, kind of an unwritten agreement has been reached that it's OK if he *reads* about it.

A: Which suggests that it's OK for him to go over to the neighbor's garage where they watch porn on an old TV set.

J: And go to church the next morning.

A: And take up the collection where everyone will see them.

J: You build all this out of a guy sitting on the can. Amazing.

A: All part of living the daily bible.

J: It really would be interesting to find out how many men are reading something uplifting or at least educational while occupied.

A: Somehow they don't seem to go together, feeding the brain while taking out the garbage.

J: Oh, there's a metaphor!

A: You know what I mean. There's a time and place for everything, and this ain't it.

J: I'm beginning to feel like an exception, an intellectual.

A: I noticed a couple of National Geographics in your basket, probably trying to impress the cleaning lady.

J: It's in keeping with your description of the bathroom, as a sanctuary. It is a private place for most men.

A: Maybe the only place where his sex fantasies can take place, maybe his only sex outlet. Judging from the obesity of a good many husbands and wives today, any real intimacy would be hard to *find* let alone experience.

J: Eating has taken over. Whole Foods has become the new church.

A: All of you sinners who are ready to be received, rise up, come forward and kneel before our bank of cash registers!

J: Oh, my. Let's go to lunch.

Death and Dying

A: I've got a cheerful topic for today.

J: OK. Let's hear it.

A: Death. Death quotes.

J: Are you kidding me?

A: Hey, what could be better than two old guys having some fun talking about dying?

J: This is fun?

A: You'll see. Here's one: "God's retirement plan is out of this world."

J: Oh, I like that. God's retirement plan is out of this world.

A: Woody Allen had one something like that: "I don't believe in the afterlife, but I'm taking a change of underwear just in case."

J: Sacrilegious.

A: But you're laughing.

J: Yes, I'm starting to get the message.

A: "A dead atheist is someone who is all dressed up with no place to go."

J: That's really good.

A: A guy named James Duffecy said that. These are all from my lady friend's collection. Here's an Irish one: "the keening is best if the corpse left money."

J: Oh, that's so Irish.

A: You probably heard a lot of that with all your Irish relatives. I experienced it once as a little kid. All the people wailing and moaning out loud. Scared the hell out of me.

J: Yes, and I'll bet all the men were in the kitchen drinking whiskey.

A: You're right. I know a couple of my uncles had a problem. Here's another: "Alas, I am dying beyond my means."

J: Oh, that's good.

A: That was Oscar Wilde. Some of these are pretty profound: "Death is the final wake-up call."

J: Wow. Perfect.

A: Doug Horton. Here's Robin Williams, "Death is nature's way of saying, 'You're table's ready.'"

J: Yes.

A: "Death is the last enemy; once we've got past that, I think everything will be all right."

J: Oh, that is terrific. Who said that?

A: A woman named Alice Thomas Ellis. "Every man dies, but not every man lives."

J: Wow. These are great.

A: A man named Sachs said that. "The fear of death keeps us from living, not dying."

J: So true.

A: That was Paul Roud. Here's an old Spanish saying, "If I die, I forgive you. If I recover, we shall see."

J: Oh, my. Of course, we picture a woman saying that.

A: Sir Walter Scott: Death. "The last sleep? No, the last awakening."

J: These are wonderful. Is that it?

A: One more: "Death is delightful. Death is dawn, the waking of a weary night of fevers unto truth and light."

J: What a great way to look at it.

A: Joaquin Miller. I probably didn't pronounce it right, and you can probably guess that I didn't bring these just to entertain you.

J: Aha. Now comes the ulterior motive.

A: Right. I thought it might be good for each of us to express how we feel about our own demise, how we accept and approach our own deaths.

J: You first.

A: I'm not looking forward to it. I feel like I'm running out of time, that I'm not going to have a chance to finish all the projects I've got underway, and that I've spent too much of my life this way and not enough of it preparing my soul for the hereafter. I want to believe that my sins are forgiven, of course, and that I will be remembered kindly by the people I've encountered. In short, I feel like I will never be ready to die.

J: I'll sound like a Pollyanna compared to that, because I am ready to die. I've lived a structured life in the cloth, long before that actually, and I have been blessed with a second life of happy matrimony and a windfall of prosperity I never dreamed of. So yes, I'm ready for that final wake-up call.

A: I guess, unfortunately, I'm more likely to take a change of underwear.

What's your purpose in life?

A: Today let's scratch away at our purpose in life.

J: OK. I've grappled with my purpose in life, at times, but I have not felt your pain. I had a good idea since the age of 12 about how I wanted to live my life. I wanted to be a priest. My father wanted me to be a priest. I accepted that early on, and just followed the path. I like to think that I've lived this precious gift of life the way it was intended. I keep trying to see the glass half-full but going deeper. We're both in our 80s, maybe not a lot of life left. If we had only three days to live, St. Aloysius would say, "keep doing what you're doing." It may sound arrogant, but there was little question about this, about where I was going, even considering the pain and grief along the way, underneath I'm satisfied that I know how to live the life I have left.

A: OK, good for you. I wish I could say that, but now, how about defining what you care about? What was your purpose? What is our purpose, now?

J: Now we're getting into philosophy. What is this? I think we can only determine it on an individual basis, where and how we spend life. The older I get, the happier I am, in many respects. I have so much to be thankful for. My buddies, when we were young, we would sit around and ask each other how we felt about things, what we thought.

A: You had some unusual buddies. Tell me how you think *now*. What is our purpose?

J: What is it? The best way? It's individual like I said. What if I asked you that question?

A: I would say that only in the last 15 years of my life, since I've been involved in Stephen Ministry, this is the first time I have had the feeling that I am doing what I was intended to do. The fact that I have a solid record of sinning and making mistakes has enabled me to be a good listener for people in trouble. I'm not judgmental, because I've been there. I would say that my goal is to care for others while I'm still struggling at this age to make a living. The Lord made it simple for us: love him and love each other.

J: There's a basic difference in finding our purpose: you, later in life; me, at an early age. But believe me, I know about sin. I didn't go into the priesthood until after high school. One time, a priest asked me if I was a good sinner, and I gave him an emphatic yes, and proceeded to back it up with the standard sin-and punishment. He said, "You think you're that powerful? The longer you stay mired in guilt, the less you will be able to face the trials ahead. If there's one thing to remember, it's that sin is past."

A: I like that part.

J: He said, "Do you think God forgives you even before you confess?" I said, "Oh no, I'd have to go to Confession first." He just looked at me and said, "God wants to forgive you more than you want to be forgiven." I think since I was ten, I wanted to be something for others, help them be the best that they could be, my purpose may have been to help people discover their purpose.

A: I would love to be able to say something like that. And to be able to carry it out as you have. You've reached thousands of people. If that priest had asked me, he might have found that my sins and mistakes were quite powerful. I hurt others, not meaning to, but hurt them in trying to find myself, and I was mired in guilt and sin and punishment from the time I was a little kid, and no, I did not feel that the Lord had forgiven me. When I faced the trial of my life, I felt that the Lord had rejected me, certainly the church rejected me, so I rejected him.

J: Painful.

A: For almost 20 years, I lived in a negative spiral, sinking into depression and near-poverty for several periods, functioning on the surface as normal. You were able to accept the sin and punishment dogma as part of the package, but it affected me, puzzled me, punished me through my high school years, Army days, college days and married life. I never really got the handle on it.

J: No way could we be recording two individuals from very different, opposite poles. When I was young, we practiced the "examination of conscience," sometime three or four times a day. Maybe that's what led me to be a psychologist. But while you were talking, I couldn't help but think that your overriding guilt was delivered by the church. When I was 40, the church banned me from Boston, and when the issue of abortion prevented me from functioning as a priest, I realized that God is much bigger than the church. This is where I stand, what I care about, to help people. Can the Bishops be wrong? Yes, of course. When I accepted the fact that they could be wrong, I discovered that I could be wrong. Since then, I've appreciated how imperfect I am, but I haven't wavered from my conscience. I haven't suffered like you. In some ways, I envy your suffering, because I do believe it leads us to a higher spiritual level.

A: You're at a pretty good level.

J: I have a lot to learn. But I am content with my purpose now. It's to take care of Mary. I think the gift we leave to others will be an example of how much two people can love one another. Together, we have tried to put the wants and needs of others before our own. As we age, it becomes more difficult. Sometimes others are putting our needs before theirs.

A: Do you think we're living the purpose that God had in mind for us? Do we really believe that God is in our lives every minute of every day?

J: Of course.

A: He didn't know that giving us free will puts the lie to that theory?

J: We can put God out of our lives whenever we want, but he is always there for us.

A: But free will trumps his plan for us? Is that it? Knowing that, why would he give us free will in the first place? Why give it to Adam and Eve? Why not just let them live out their lives in Paradise, and all the rest of us in our own paradise?

J: Probably because we are even happier when we overcome our problems.

A: We probably cause most of our problems.

J: Probably.

Where is God
in all this?

A: You know, we take a look at all the problems throughout the world, the financial crisis, the wasteful wars in Iraq and Afghanistan, tsunamis, earthquakes, just to name a few, and we ask, "Where is God in all this?"

J: He's right here. Look, I'm eighty-eight. My first eighty years did not prepare me for my most recent eight years. Together, we may be members of Tom Brokaw's Greatest Generation, but we are not Gurus. We are just two guys in conversation about the issues and God. You are the more practical one; I'm more theoretical. Your having driven a taxi in New York and similar wild things I may have wanted to do, but never did, mark us as different, but often times the same in our thinking. We cannot solve the problems, maybe just open up some more of our thinking. We are not famous celebrities, but we can help others to cope.

A: Fair enough.

J: So, "Where is God in all this?" First, I could not live for one minute without my faith in God, in facing today's abuses of power. The chaff and wheat. The Lord says Let them grow together, we'll separate them at harvest and burn the chaff."

A: You're evading the question.

J: Of course. I started to say, we are not born in sin, we are born in . . .

A: Wait, we are not born in sin?

J: No way. We are born in goodness, the goodness that spills over when God created the universe. He, or she, is the loving source.

A: We were instructed as children to believe that we were born in sin. Sin and punishment has guided my life. Just contrast that with establishing a personal relationship with God.

J: God doesn't stand still. As the source of all change, he helps us evolve, makes sure we can grapple with our problems. God is freedom. He frees man to turn bad into good, good into bad. Crooks get away with murder, because this is a free society. Options that the Creator provides often turned into greed, witness the bailouts rewarding the perpetrators.

A: All this begs the question, "Why did God give us free will?" He provided this great universe, in perfect balance, covering all man's needs. He says just love me and love your neighbor, and we respond by preparing other countries to annihilate their neighbors. We are the world's leading supplier of weapons. We talked about this before, but what did the Lord have in mind with free will?

J: To become the fullest human beings possible, realizing our potentials and to leave the world in better shape than when we came into it. God is, first, the source of all love.

Our purpose is to overcome the greed, lust and deceit of the world.

A: With our free will? Overcome the greed and lust? We're human beings, with weakness. Our free will leads us to greed and lust. Granted, man can do good, man can make a difference, and he is expected to contribute. Goodness can overcome fear and prejudice and all that, but the reality is that man is going to stumble and fall, and today he is continuously reassured by the mainstream media that he can have it all, especially money and sex.

J: You mentioned the media before. When media is controlled by the very few, it could be that Americans are the worst informed. Not that we don't get enough news, but it's filtered. Spin. Deceit, as orchestrated by the likes of Rupert Murdoch.

A: His mouthpieces, Karl Rove, Rush Limbaugh, and Glenn Beck and their wrecking crews.

J: How did we become so prejudiced? Were we born evil? No.

A: Almost born evil. Witness the dominating father, or mother.

J: Violence grows out of prejudice.

A: Free will at its worst.

J: Look at the Roman empire. In the name of peace, they took over the minds of the people.

A: Not unlike today.

J: Prejudice! Starts in the home, spreads to the neighborhood, school, church. We grew up in a Catholic versus Protestant neighborhood.

A: Me, too. We weren't allowed to play basketball in the Protestant school's gym. Not prevented by the Protestants, but by our church. Love your neighbor.

J: The Lord asks us to partner with him, to respect the needs of others, to create a kingdom on earth as it is in Heaven.

A: That's a reach.

We need a Leader

A: OK, we've touched on the Lord's "love me and love one another" and concluded that as his children we've pretty much let him down.

J: We have the choice of following a dictator or the Lord. Hussein for example.

A: Or Bush for example. The Axis of Evil.

J: Absolutely. John the Baptist was regarded as the greatest prophet prior to God's kingdom on earth, but after him, a child would be regarded as greater. Let's go back to the concept of evil and sin on the one hand, contrasted with love and beauty on the other. Or, power versus love. Power leads to violence, greed.

A: So far, so good.

J: Men in our prison system would paint the word love on the four fingers of the left hand and the word hate on the four fingers of the right. Today we have separation of church and state. Jesus answered, "render unto Caesar that which is Caesar's, to God that which is God's." People of the time were told to vote against their conscience and couldn't do it. I'm much more hopeful than you. I believe that when the world comes to an end, there will be more good than bad. Caesar abused his power, Bush his. Accepting misuse of power by prophets and leaders is easy. I believe our mission is to do good.

A: OK, but where are we? Following Caesar? How can you be so hopeful in face of world conditions today? Starting in the US?

J: I really believe, now this may sound strange, that evil has its tail, and that the tail will snap! Look around, see all these people who have amassed fortunes and are not happy. Money is not just compulsive, but corrosive. History of institutions and countries has shown a pattern of growth, power, control and demise.

A: America now.

J: Not pretty.

A: So, as long as we believe in God, in goodness, we will overcome?

J: The vast majority of people on earth are good. The problem is that those in power make themselves appear as good.

A: OK, but since the time of Jesus, man has gone astray. We've advanced in technology, but we haven't kept pace with goodness.

J: Technology could have been used for good. And is, to a great extent, but look, there are probably ten times as many people on earth now as there were when we were born. How did most make a living? By subsistence farming. They're faceless, they eke out a living. Power. When we say every advance leads to power and power leads to abuse, what we may be asking, " is man dedicated to creating a better world or is he taken up with *me first*?"

A: OK. Subsistence farming still exists in the third world, but disappearing. Africa, for example, where the poor are also plagued with Aids and genocide. Are you saying that only the poor will see Heaven? I'm hopeful, of course, but I'm also a realist. You could say that the people of Jesus' time anticipated that the end of the world, Perousia, was just around the corner, a couple of generations away, but today countries do have the capability to take us out in a hurry. What if Osama Bin Laden has a nuclear arsenal in his cave in the mountains?

J: I believe that we have 30, 50, 100 years before that eventuality. When the Romans commercialized the farms, the little people no longer had any power. But one by one, they were able to bring down the empire. Violence is not the answer, but the individual is the key. The majority of the people are good.

A: So how do we get power in the hands of all these good people? They aren't 100% good. Look at today's election process; Rove and his ilk put a spin on any and all chinks in the armor of the opponent, right now painting Obama as a Muslim and a revolutionary Weatherman, certainly not an American like us. Why aren't all these good people rising up? All these good, poor people who have been brainwashed by consumerism, fear and prejudice.

J: It won't work until people are willing to die on the cross.

A: Are you kidding me? Die on the cross? In this day and age? How are we going to reach people? You and I are going to provide the example? You a former priest and me a screw up? I'm not ready to die on the cross. Enough that I have faith in Jesus and can find some peace of mind from time to time.

J: I was born into a very religious family, the Catechism, everything. My beliefs were established, rock solid before I was 15 years old. I knew that there was this guy who came down here, started with a small group of fishermen and built a church that now numbers in the millions. He was an illiterate day laborer, and he surrounded himself with people just like you and me and connected them with the Lord. You and I can't be Jesus, but we can follow his example. That's what you are doing with your life, being there for people in trouble. Yes, one by one.

A: I'd like to believe that's possible.

J: Unless we are willing to die for the truth. I am willing right now, because I want to be free.

A: Free, as in feeling an inner peace?

J: Yes. Once we sell our soul, we're owned by someone else. Jesus was a revolutionary without violence. What is it that makes life worthwhile? Families willing to sacrifice. There is so much good underneath despair. But people are seduced by those in power. Let the sharks in. Bush stole the election, set himself up as the Decider, with no restrictions by an inept Congress. Look where that has led us.

A: We need a leader.

J: Now.

A: Do we believe that only the poor inherit the earth? And do we want it, is one question. We are surrounded in this community by thousands of very wealthy people who own grand homes and several cars and attend church regularly and complete Bible studies by the dozen. But unfortunately, they're not poor. Too bad.

J: Well, we'll see, now that we're heading into a Depression or at least where a great many are going to lose some of that wealth. I'm glad they're going to church. When we were kids, it was a mortal sin to miss mass on Sunday. Straight to hell if you got hit by a car. Especially bad if you weren't wearing clean underwear.

A: My brothers and I used to shudder kneeling in the pews waiting to go into the confessional and having to confess our grievous sins like saying hell or damn. But, again how do we reach people like you and me, only younger? How do we get back to loving God and loving each other?

J: Who was the leader in South America who wanted all his people to have transistor radios? Ferrara? Anyway, it didn't work, because he couldn't control the radio stations. Maybe the wealthy have to show by example. Bill Gates, people like that. It goes back to one-to-one. Just today, at the pool, I was able to encourage a man who had lost his job. Paul said, "See those Christians? They love each other."

A: We know that there a lot of people out there experiencing real trouble. We have to reach out to each other, like you say, one-to-one.

J: We wandered all over today, but one thing is clear. We need a leader.

Good Old Days

A: I was reading an article in the Atlantic that got me thinking about the good old days.

J: Yes and no. Good old days, I mean.

A: When people got married first, then lived together. When life expectancy, just 100 years ago, was 47 years.

J: Wow. 47. Today we're just getting started.

A: In Jesus' time, old age was in the 30s.

J: That's something to think about.

A: But in our early years, only eight percent of the population had telephones.

J: Party lines, with people listening in on other conversations. Today we have the internet making those conversations available all over the world.

A: Fourteen percent were still without a bathtub.

J: Phew! We both remember coal stoves in the living rooms.

A: Do you think people were more spiritual in those days? Or more religious?

J: Oh-oh. I feel a trap coming on. I'll guess religious.

A: No trap. I'm asking.

J: I'd say religious. I think more people said their prayers, went to church, and feared God outright than they do today.

A: Go to the head of the class. Feared God, especially.

J: God, the loving source of all goodness, was the be and being of all things from plants and flowers to man and woman. His sheer goodness created all nature. Man has wasted a lot of it, and maybe we could have been self-sufficient back then, instead of being dependent on oil as we are today.

A: Exxon just reported a $14 billion profit for 3rd quarter.

J: Maybe one day we'll have windmills instead of wars.

A: Do you think man is capable of bringing this about?

J: You are more realistic than I. I'm more hopeful, on the creative side.

A: Whoa, I've always been considered creative and optimistic. I've been kicked in the shins a few times, but I still have hope. I ask if today's societies, who are easily divided by lies and deceits, are capable of bringing about a semblance of the balance God gave us in the first place?

J: When I look back, I see that life was good. In the priesthood for 38 years, I was saved from a lot of the trials and troubles others have experienced. Maybe I was too sheltered. That's why I consider my later years working in the prison system as so important.

A: You're dancing around my question, so I guess that's a no. But your years working with prisoners, and guards, brings us to ask if God intended this or that to happen. Was that in God's plan back when you were studying to be a priest? Is all this in God's plan?

J: Here we go again.

·A: God gave us a world, or universe, in perfect balance, providing everything man needs. So why did he give us free will, knowing that we would screw things up, as in today's lust for power and money, the greed of the hedge fund managers and the financial chaos now affecting markets around the world? Are we saying that God planned all this, that he's up there moving the chess men around on a giant board?

J: No. How God works in our lives will always be a mystery. Let's try to explore where we are, where man in general is, in today's world.

A: Great idea.

J: I like to think that man is on two parallel journeys: one, technology and two, relationships. One, of course, is the internet, computer, laptops, cell phones, television, radios, cars, airplanes, medical, all of that. Two is man to man and woman, husband-wife, family, neighbors, communities, countries.

A: OK, so far.

J: As never before, there is a universal connectivity available; we can communicate instantly. We no longer have an excuse for not understanding one another, or for learning how to get along with all different cultures. Blogging, for example, is available to everyone, uncensored, extemporary, open to criticism as well as persuasion. How will we use it universally? We have chosen to waste lives and billions of dollars each month on unwinnable "wars" a product of people in control who cover their actions with manipulations of truth.

A: I think I'm hearing that it would be wonderful if man could instead put his technology to work in improving relationships, around the world.

J: Something like that.

Making a Living

A: Your history of employment is easy to understand. Mine is all over the lot. A few assignments here and there for a few months, one for almost two years, but most were for a few days, and then only as a spokesman.

J: You were always free-lancing?

A: After I lost my business, yes.

J: Up and down. Off and on.

A: Yes. Exactly. I may have picked up some of that from my father. When I was a kid, he was living from assignment to assignment as a sign painter. I painted the backs of many signs. He let me be his helper.

J: How did he learn that trade?

A: That's a long story. He came over from the old country when he was eleven years old, along with his brother who was nine. It was not unusual in those times for the parents to send the kids over first; that somehow made it easier for the parents to cut through some of the red tape. That's another story: picture these two kids waiting on the dock at Ellis

Island for the guy who was supposed to meet them, who instead took the money and went to Florida.

J: Wow.

A: A family they had met on the boat took them to Niagara Falls. They lived with them for two years in an apartment above a drug store. Picture these two Jewish boys going to mass with their new family. His brother later became a dentist, but Rudy, my father, dropped out of high school and went to work in a department store. He was doing the window displays, counter displays, and signs. Working there, he became a real dude: those were the high collar days, and he had an eye for the ladies. He took note of this one fair-haired, tiny-wasted young lady getting off the street car each morning, and before long he found a way to get acquainted. She turned out to be my mother, an Irish Roman Catholic girl from a large Irish Catholic family named Carney in a village to the North named Lewiston.

J: Really?

A: When the family first met him at a picnic, she introduced him as Billy instead of his real name, Rudy. It stuck, of course, but each of us boys, as we in turn became of age, wondered why everyone called our father Uncle Billy. Her father had died in his early 40s, and my mother always described how enterprising he was, building a huge stable behind the barn to house the farmers' horses overnight when they would bring their crops to market. We didn't learn the whole story until half a century later when the Niagara Falls Gazette ran a four-page feature in the rotogravure section commemorating a Lewiston landmark, describing the First and Last Chance Tavern, run by Francis Carney.

J: Oh, that's good.

A: An interesting sidelight, my father's father also ran a tavern in Austria, well, they called it an Inn, that featured an outdoor bowling alley, kind of a bocce ball with pins. So you can see that I have reason to be proud of my heritage.

J: Let's have a drink on that.

A: Anyway, back to the heritage of working on an assignment basis. Rudy did work for a big sign company during the Roaring 20s, but then came the market crash and then the Depression. We were poor, like you, during those years, and I remember how happy he was when he got an order to paint a series of signs for the WPA and the NRA, all red, white and blue. One was a banner that stretched across Delaware Avenue, our main street, a feature of the Fourth of July Parade. He decorated my tricycle wheels with red, white and blue crepe paper, and I joined a contingent of at least 30 other kids in the parade. Or so it seemed. Probably 10 or 12.

J: Things were simpler then.

A: When he did get an assignment, it would be something no one else would do, like lettering one of those factory smoke stacks reaching 100 feet in the air, or a water tower or one of the big freighters in Buffalo Harbor. Then at night he would letter paper signs for the windows of the butcher store or bakery (Rye Bread 6c). I can see him now. He had built a large easel behind the furnace, and I'd sit there on a stool watching these beautiful letters appear on the blank paper. Fathers worked hard in those days. They were family men.

J: You told me once that your father wasn't religious. But he was spiritual.

A: Well, he would probably get a laugh out of that. He was good-natured. loved to kid. And he was humble. I would be with him once in a while when we would go into the bank on the corner, the First National with big imposing pillars out front, because he had gotten a great assignment, like a new storefront sign for a local merchant. Suddenly I would see my father in a whole different light, with hat in hand, literally, seeking a loan (factoring, they called it) in order to buy the materials he would need. The banker, a real stuffed shirt who took up the collection in church, would look down his nose at this man in coveralls, paint-splattered coveralls at that, but when we left, my Dad would be so happy, and we'd stop for an ice cream cone on the way home.

J: That's what I mean by spiritual.

A: Just down the street from the bank was the barber shop run by Nick the Greek. Three barbers full-time in this little town, along with a shoe shine boy who was really a bookie, and everybody knew it, including the cop out front whose sole duty was to see that the school kids got safely across the street four times a day.

J: That's so America. The stuffy banker and the friendly barber shop.

A: "Make sure you tell the barber to cut it short." Those were the instructions from my mother every time we were sent to the barber's. It wasn't always fun for us for another reason. In later life, I began to realize that it was a focal point for local gossip. Many times, Nick would ask me, as he had my three brothers before me, "Say, kid, they tell me your father was born in Austria, right, he was Jewish?" I would tell him I didn't know, because I didn't. I had never thought about it. But if I had a nickel for every time I was asked that question in our Republican, Protestant town, I would be a rich man.

J: Irish mother, Jewish father. Abe's Irish Rose.

A: See? He was not a Jewish father. He was born a Jewish boy, but the only time he set foot in a Temple in America was for a wedding or funeral.

J: Ah. You're still sensitive to that.

A: Of course. I am very aware of prejudice. I worried for Obama right up to the last minute. My oldest brother came close to becoming a priest. There was never a danger of that with me, but I make the point, because my mother was never really accepted into the Ladies Sodality. They made her feel like less of a Catholic. My brothers and I felt the same attitudes, even though we played on the church teams. Our basketball team could not play the Presbyterian team, because our pastor would not allow us to enter their building.

J: Your background is rich. Mine, too. We have an opportunity to explore in depth some of the crazy things you and I and our fathers, particularly, experienced during the Great Depression years. We may be on the threshold of another one, and people in today's generations have no idea of what to expect. I was born in 1920. I grew up a poor kid in Bridgeport, Connecticut during the Roaring 20s. Then came the market crash in 1929, and we learned what it meant to be really poor. My father worked at the bank at the time, but let me go back: he had worked in a factory, Remington Arms, from age 13 until the time he met my mother. She had been doing office work at the bank and managed to get my father an interview there. He started there as an assistant janitor, and he used to like to say, "I started as a draftsman. I opened and closed the windows."

A: That's where you get your story-telling.

J: Well, not so much. My mother was better at that, but my father was my hero. His father had been an alcoholic who deserted the family, so my father and his mother became the sole support of the five kids. They lived in what we would call a shack and were often on welfare. For a time they washed their clothes in a small stream. In the summer, they walked to the shore and dug for clams. My father showed me where they would wait for the coal trains to go by, spilling coal where the track curved. That was their fuel for the coal stove. In the morning, they took turns dressing in front of the stove. They'd go down to the dairy with pails, and scoop up the fragments of ice that the trucks left behind. We have no concept today of how our ancestors lived.

A: We see pictures of people starving in Africa and third-world countries, and even then it's hard for us to relate.

J: My father lived a structured life for his last 35 years. They were grateful that he had a steady job even through the Depression years. At least they had food on the table. But he had no use for his father. I wasn't really aware of that until one time when I was nine years old, he asked me if I wanted to go with him to visit his father. I jumped at the chance, figuring they must have had a relationship like ours. During the ride, he set the record straight, starting with, "I hate my father."

A: I'll bet that was a shock.

J: When I asked why, he asked me, "Did you ever see me hit your Mother? Did I ever hit you? Did you ever see me come staggering down the street, the kids throwing snowballs at the old drunk?"

A: Wow.

J: My father was always grateful that he had security. When the crash came, he lost the little extra he had in the market, but he knew he was better off than the people around him. And he liked wearing a tie to work.

A: Did you have brothers or sisters?

J: A little sister. She was a really a cousin, one of another five kids whose father left them, but we grew up together as brother and sister. Three women in my early life: my mother, her sister and my little sister. When I got old enough, and one night when the dinner was finished, I got up enough nerve to ask, "Can I go in the living room now with Daddy?"

A: It's different today. Very few families have dinner together. Everybody's going in different directions. Maybe the tough times ahead will bring back some of what's been missing.

J: Yes. Families tend to stay together in tough times. . .

A: And we hope that extends to countries.

J: . . . families listened to the radio and laughed together. Amos 'n Andy.

A: Oops. We didn't know we were reinforcing stereotypes, prejudices with that one.

J: Maybe the point we're making . . .

A: We started out talking about employment, and now we've really talked about our fathers and Depression times.

J: Which is OK. We're on the doorstep of another Great Depression.

A: What message can we leave for the next generations?

J: Yes. What have we learned that applies?

A: Maybe it's as simple as saying tough times enable us to see more clearly what is really important.

J: How do we even suggest the kind of sacrifice ahead? The current generations have never experienced anything like it.

A: Tough times bring us back to our relationships. With family. God.

Stunt Man

J: You must have some stories from your part-time acting career.

A: Those were fun, for the most part. Trying to break into the field wasn't fun, but you get great rewards for your efforts. I still get residual checks, enough to cover my coffee habit at Dunkin Donuts.

J: I'm listening.

A: One night I got a call from a lady friend who was working as a production assistant on a major movie. They needed a stand-in for James Coburn who had the lead in a Dashiell Hammett turkey called The Dain Curse. The movie was destined for television, would run for three consecutive nights, two hours each night.

J: That's a long movie.

A: Yeah. I don't know anybody who sat through it. If you're familiar with Dashiell Hammett, you know that he introduced a new character every third paragraph and a new plot twist on every page, so you can imagine how convoluted the movie got.

J: I didn't see it, but just what did you do as a stand-in?

A: Just that. You stand-in for the actor back in the trailer studying his lines, and you walk through his moves as the Director sets up the scene. The crew sets up the lighting, the sound, all that on *you,* then Coburn steps in and delivers. After a couple of weeks, I got to know just how he would handle the moves. It was fun, and I learned a lot.

J: What a kick. How long were you involved?

A: The whole three months. It was a great experience. Antique cars, old houses, you know, set in the roaring 20s, in an old town on Shelter Island, way out on the tip of Long Island. The really fun part was doing Coburn's stunts, most of which fell apart, because the guy planning the stunts was not really a stunt coordinator, just one of the grips filling in.

J: You did the stunts?

A: Yeah. At one point Coburn, me, is inching his way, back to the wall, toward a window where he can get a peek at the bad guys inside, when there's this big explosion blowing out the sides of the wall and sending Coburn over the railing and into a net below, which meant, of course, that I had to time my dive to coincide with the explosion.

J: Whooeee.

A: Fortunately for me, the amateur stunt coordinator came close to blowing out the wall in setting it up, and they abandoned the scene. Similar thing happened when I was supposed to fall off the running board and roll down an embankment. I was ready, but the Director decided that Coburn wouldn't be on the running board in the first place.

J: When was all this taking place?

A: In the roaring 20s. Oh, you mean the movie. 1977. I was in my 40s when I launched my second career, actually my third or fourth, I lost track.

J: So you ended up not doing any stunts?

A: Oh, no. There were several others. In one scene, they had me playing an Oriental type bad guy, all made up, full robe, standing on a pedestal, who gets riddled with machine gun bullets, blood spouting out from the special vest inside the robe. Actually ketchup. The only problem was, the stunt guy had set the vest inside out and all the jets sent the jolts into my chest. There was real blood and hell to pay.

J: Yipes! I bet that hurt.

A: Only when I smiled. But meanwhile I had done some other stunts, falling down stairs after being shot, dodging between old cars on the move, stuff like that. It was fun. And three months work! For an actor, that was a plum.

J: You earned your money.

A: It was a great learning experience, how they set up the lighting, how actors never look at the camera. I did some crazy commercials, too. One time I was booked to do one in Indiana for a manufacturer of roofing materials, dressed as a lion tamer, think circus, standing on the roof, flailing my whip at the lions below, taming the insulation problems I guess.

J: So what happened?

A: Well I arrived, expecting to find the set in a large studio somewhere, but no, we were shooting in a neighborhood on a real house, on a slanted roof, you know, ideal for the view from down below, but not so safe for the lion tamer up above. We ended up with a rope around my middle, concealed of course, tied to a chimney.

J: I wish I could have been there to see that.

A: It was fun. A cheering crowd had assembled, and they felt like they were part of the production. The producer had spread the word that a New York actor who was on the soap One Life to Live was coming to shoot a commercial. I was a celebrity.

J: You were famous.

A: I did a whole bunch of bit parts, I mean bits. They call them under-fives. Under five lines. Like being an extra, only your five lines help strengthen the scene in some way. Great for your ego, to be able to say, "I was the bartender in that scene with Dustin Hoffman."

J: I can see how young actors get swayed.

A: That's for sure. It's a tough business, because in some ways, there's no reward quite like it. In other ways, there's no frustration quite like it. When I was working at it, remember I didn't start until I was in my forties, and I was a free-lancer in my other work so I was used to the ups and downs of life, but just think: there were 60,000 actors ready to work for a few hundred total assignments, in the entire country. Not jobs, just a few days, or hours, work.

J: Wow. All those kids from Iowa and Kansas coming to the big city to strike it rich in the movies. Or Broadway. To be discovered.

A: Because they could sing and loved to dance.

J: I suppose most returned home heartbroken. And broke.

A: A lot of them stay. Settle for waitress jobs, double up in tiny apartments in areas where their parents would have a stroke to find them.

J: I'd guess that a lot of them come from broken homes or at least situations they want to escape from.

A: That's probably accurate. Would make an interesting statistic. Most that I met are just star struck. They go back home and somehow get to college or get married and settle down.

J: But at least they tried, and they gained some experience, some tough lessons and probably some high points they can take back home and talk about for the rest of their lives.

A: Oddly enough, they probably won't talk about it too much.

J: Really?

A: Kind of a closed chapter. If people find out, they say, "You were an actor? What were you in?" If it wasn't a movie they had seen in the last year and you weren't in a starring role, they give you kind of a condescending look that says, "Oh, then you weren't a real actor."

J: I don't know about that. I think most of us are envious. We'd like to be able to say we were in a movie, even for a moment on camera, in the background already.

A: I think the heartbreak and futility of that time in your life takes over your recall. You kind of enjoy a quiet moment with the high points once in a while, but it's pretty much a closed chapter.

J: Interesting. But I'm still impressed. My friend was an actor.

The Audience
writes the script

A: Did you use a lot of metaphors and analogies in your talks?

J: Did I ever.

A: The audience remembers the metaphors, right?

J: Right. The metaphors connect with something they already accept with a better way to remember it. You have given them something valuable, memorable they can add to their arsenal. They're grateful, and you have earned their respect.

A: Quotations, the same way.

J: You bet. We don't have to be brilliant, just quote brilliant people.

A: They've already done the thinking.

J: When you know or can sense how your audience feels, then you can connect your feelings to theirs and theirs to yours.

A: I tried to get that point across in my workshops: it all starts with the audience. Their point of view. I'd try to tell these CEOs that it's not about them. I'd tell them that whenever someone asked them to be a speaker, they should ask for an audience breakdown, to determine where they are coming from, their attitudes, their hot buttons.

J: That's so basic, but so many times speakers ignore it and then wonder why they laid an egg.

A: I had one guy who learned that lesson. He was delivering his standard speech for doctors when he suddenly realized he was talking to nurses, some of them male.

J: It's the audience's point of view that matters; then in your planning, you know which quotes to feature, which analogies. Later, when you deliver them and see all the heads nodding agreement, it's a wonderful feeling. You've got 'em in the palm of your hand.

A: We quote Socrates and the audience puts you right up there with all the learned.

J: Learned. "Knowing things makes you learned; knowing yourself makes you wise." That's a quote I used a lot. We could be accused of manipulating the minds of those in the audience, using a technique to reinforce our own convictions and plant them on the unwary.

A: As in religion.

J: There you go again. But yes, people who know how the mind works, its insulas and cingulated cortices.

A: Right. I got the part about insulated cornices, but cingulated?

J: Not even close.

A: Back down to earth. I understand manipulating the minds of the audience. The media surrounds us with it. At one time, I was writing copy, and slogans, for Miller Beer.

J: That's bringing it down to earth all right.

A: Tell me the difference between a metaphor and an analogy.

J: Wait. I'm going to look it up.

Six years in
the Slammer

A: Tell me again about the time you went to prison.

J: That's the way I'd put it to people. I'd say, "Don't fool with me. I spent six years in the slammer."

A. Behind a desk?

J: Not exactly. No, those were some of the most rewarding years of my life, working with the prisoners.

A: Is that what brought you down here?

J: Yes. They needed a Chief Psychologist at Central Prison. Sixteen hundred inmates, a hundred seven on death row. I had my hands full.

A: It wasn't depressing?

J: Oh, hell yes! The first time you go through the sally ports, you know, that's where they slam that heavy metal door behind you, and now there's another heavy metal door in front of you, and you stand there on-camera for what seems like an hour while the guards are determining whether or not you will go through more sally ports or back out the gate.

A: That's an experience.

J: It was a challenge. But here was a chance to make a real difference in people's lives. My job, my goal was to improve the mental health of the inmates so they would retain as much humanity as they could under abnormally brutal circumstances. I used to tell Mary that my job was to assure that the men on death row keep whatever mental health and stability they have so they can be executed.

A: Cheerful thought.

J: I found that the prison system hasn't advanced much since the Civil War days, but there were some unforgettable people working with the prisoners. Sam, the Warden, big guy, six foot five, about 250 pounds, and tough, nobody dared cross him, but he was fair and he could be almost gentle, even dealing with some guy who had lost it completely.

A: I can't imagine how anyone could stay in that job for any length of time.

J: That's right. After I left, that's when I had the heart attack after six years, he was promoted, started drinking again and died, just a shell of the man he had been.

A: Is the prison system really that bad?

J: While I was recuperating, I had a lot of time to think about how churches, schools, prisons, corporations, governments, all kinds of institutions, keep following systems that were set up originally for attaining worthy goals, but eventually got off track.

A: Don't keep up with changing times?

J: Old systems are like old people who get set in their ways. It doesn't do much good to hide criminals in prisons, you know, out of sight out of mind, and do little or nothing about the problems in society that contribute to their lawlessness.

A: You make a case for rehabilitating them? You think that's feasible?

J: Rehab presupposes habilitation. Most inmates were never habilitated in the first place. I say put half the money we now spend on prisons into preschool programs and beef up grades K through five, cut class size, pay teachers who work with difficult kids a better wage, and enable dysfunctional families to learn how to live in society.

A: And you call me an idealist.

J: And you keep saying we have no choice but to make it happen.

A: How do we reach the politicians?

J: Now, there's hypocrisy. Politicians play on the public's irrational fear of crime, which as you point out is fanned by the media machine, and they promise, "If you elect me, I'll clean up the streets, throw everybody in the can, then you and your wife and kids can walk the streets safely again."

A: Prisons don't really change behaviors, do they?

J: No way. You can't change behaviors until you change the way people perceive themselves. Inmates are there against their will, they don't like the other inmates, or the staff, and they have little motivation to improve their cognition or attitudes.

A: Out of sight out of mind wins over facing up to the problem.

J: As in so many of our institutions.

A: Congress, corporations.

J: Remember the CEOs of the tobacco companies standing up and swearing in court that they didn't believe their companies were manipulating the amount of nicotine in their cigarettes and they didn't believe nicotine was harmful to people's health.

A: Don't forget their generosity in World War Two when they issued a carton of cigarettes every month to every soldier. Of course, that had nothing to do with building demand for their product.

J: Anyway, the prison system needs a lot of work. I'm happy I was able to get through to a good many inmates.

Pain and pleasure

A: Some of the old formula is still featured in the worship service today.

J: Oh-oh. Here it comes.

A: Think about it. We still see God as the force up there doling out all kinds of punishment down here.

J: Yes. There's some of that.

A: Some? It's featured. Fear is the word, and punishment is the weapon. You get out of line, and God is going to make you pay for it. That's the message.

J: You've got to admit that it's a pretty effective formula.

A: You bet. Then in the next breath, we feature a loving God. Evidently, he loves us so much that if we don't do what we're told, he scrolls down in his database of punishment and selects a couple of whoppers that will get our attention.

J: You're saying that fear is the underlying force of religion. That's a given.

A: It's at odds with a loving God.

J: Yes. But it's not unlike a parent.

A: We take away the car if our kid gets a ticket for speeding. We're taught how to punish people by religion?

J: You could say that.

A: God said "love me and love each other." He didn't say, "Punish your kids the way I punish you."

J: We keep coming back here to fear as the motivator.

A: Right. It's taken me a long time, all my life, to get beyond the guilt and punishment ritual that was ingrained at an early age. I don't want to see God at this point as the guy up there with the great sword ready to smote us into oblivion.

J: You have a better motivator?

A: Mine doesn't work. It's God's, actually. The *love* one another.

J: We don't love our neighbors? Like Iran?

A: Hear me out. We go to church, worship service, and we sing the hymns up there on the big screen, "He gives and takes away, he gives and takes away," over and over again. Then the preacher gives us an enlightening recap of how God appeared before Ezekial and directed him to go over there and annihilate the Slovakians, because they didn't prepare the offering with motzah balls.

J: They deserved to be annihilated.

A: Then he hammers home the point that God gives us pain and God gives us pleasure.

J: Well, that ain't half bad.

A: He's up there doling it out. That's the point.

J: You don't like that.

A: Right. I can't abide by that.

J: And yet you can't come up with a better formula.

A: For me, yes. For the rest of the world, no.

J: Shoot.

A: You've heard it before. I don't think we should see God as up there doling out punishment, or pain or pleasure. I want to see God as a loving God. He gives us life on a planet that has everything we need to live a peaceful life together. Then he gives us free will and we proceed to screw things up. The way we use it creates our own pain or pleasure.

J: I like that.

A: Good.

J: But it isn't Biblical.

A: That's for sure.

The Man-Woman Relationship

A: How about today we talk some more about the man-woman relationship?

J: There's lots to talk about.

A: With all the influence of television, and now the internet, the basic, honest romance idea is replaced by sex. There is no build-up of the respect and trust Nouwen talks about, as the foundation of a good relationship.

J: I hear you.

A: No real exchange of personal experiences, the reasons we think the way we do. The mistakes, the triumphs, you know, the aha moments of discovery, maybe even redemption.

J: The discoveries, that what we seek is elusive but must include an understanding of, and a willingness to accept one another's faults and peculiarities.

A: Not ours, of course.

J: What we really seek is a partner on the same spiritual path. Not holier than thou, simply one who has experienced similar successes and failures and thus has a better idea of what to look for the next time around.

A: Right, and that may explain why there are so many third tries, the twice divorced. Me, for example. They, I, were too vulnerable after the first breakup to recognize the red flags in the second relationship, too eager to jump in bed with this wonderful substitute who would fulfill all the missing ingredients of acceptance and affection and maybe just plain attention.

J: I've seen it where those who were not so vulnerable welcomed the attention of someone quite different from the first mate, as long as the physical gratification was included, and gradually gave in, or just the opposite, ended the relationship, realizing that it was never really fulfilling and moved on to another relationship of the same nature, ultimately deciding that marriage was not the answer, or ending up marrying one who had been filling in as kind of a step-mother housekeeper.

A: Or becoming a sour single old man. There's evidence all around us that some of us get married for the wrong reasons in the first place and repeat the mistakes the second time around. We marry the same person twice, so to speak, because we are so vulnerable. We think we have found the conditions missing in the first. The attention, affection and sex.

J: Then we find that it's temporary, offered willingly at first to cement the relationship.

A: And soon relegated to the back burner.

J: What we might welcome instead are the relationships considered strange, like the one you told me about. An elderly man, I put it politely, meeting with a younger woman, one who could be his daughter, where respect and trust are a given, with no ulterior motives aimed toward the bedroom, just two people who have gone through similar trials, broken relationships that once were meaningful.

A: Two people who can meet over coffee and be open and honest with one another, and if that bonding makes room for our Maker, all the better. In that kind of relationship, there is no reluctance to talk about the conditions of their trial.

J: No embarrassment to include descriptions or maybe acknowledge that the Lord wasn't in their lives at the time.

A: Yes. Those over-coffee sessions are probably more spiritual, because they're more honest, more apt to include the Lord than we might find in a religious setting.

J: I accept that, even though I, as a priest, met with a few young ladies.

A: No offense, but I think God is missing in most marriages. He is part of the wedding ceremonies as kind of representative from outer space. He is acknowledged in the priest's, or minister's soliloquy. Once we accept this stamp of approval, the couple is considered married for life.

J: You and I have learned that a real marriage requires active participation on the part of God himself. We know he is always there for us, but we are too busy before the wedding with all the preparations, and too busy after, inventorying all the presents and getting back to work.

A: What we need is some down-to-earth third party counseling.

J: Along with some help from above.

A: Amen to that.

Going Soloveitchik

A: Ever hear of a guy named Soloveitchik?

J: Is this a trick question?

A: No trick. He was a Jewish theologian. I figured you Jesuits would be kind enough to include his wild perceptions in your hallowed dogma.

J: Oh, that Soloveitchik. Sounded like some chick singing a solo in your old neighborhood.

A: Ours was a pure white Protestant neighborhood. We were the only family for miles with a Jewish-sounding name.

J: Ours was a mix of Italian and Irish with a few other foreigners thrown in.

A: No Blacks?

J: A few, but they stayed mostly in their own neighborhood.

A: Ours, too. There was one Black in our graduating class. We played other schools in our district that were mostly Black, or a good mix of other ethnics. I didn't really get to know any until I went in the Army, and they were mostly segregated even then.

J: I'd like to think we've made great strides, but if it weren't for sports on television, and the rock stars on television, they'd still be fighting for survival.

A: Yes! Now they dominate the sports world, especially basketball with these giants slamming down dunks, controlling the backboards. Football, too, these huge linemen, and backs that can run like deer.

J: But on with Soloveitchik.

A: Somebody referenced him in an article I was reading, probably in the Atlantic, but anyway, his theory was that there are two moral universes. You could probably come up with a few more.

J: I could try.

A: He called them Adam One and Adam Two.

J: Back to square one, or two.

A: Adam One is knee deep in his own problems and competes in building the world around him.

J: Like most of us.

A: Adam Two is spiritual, overwhelmed by the universe, a spectator and worshiper.

J: Not many of those around. Thoreau, maybe, at Walden Pond.

A: Well, *you* would qualify, but I guess that's the point he makes, along with others.

J: That most of us are Adam One with a touch of Adam Two.

A: Right. Go to church on Sunday.

J: Not many of us who can say they live solely for Jesus.

A: Amen to that. But I thought it might be appropriate for us to talk about, because most of us get more interested in the spiritual as we prepare to leave the real world here for the real world there.

J: Who was it that said, "It's difficult to live a spiritual life. People think there's something wrong with you," or words to that effect.

A: Maybe that's what Solo is saying. We'll have to Google him. That the best we can do is live each day doing what has to be done on the outside and carry out the spiritual on the inside.

J: As long as we're demonstrating the inside on the outside.

A: Yeah, *reflecting* the spiritual. Easier said than done.

J: I would guess that most people avoid showing their spiritual side.

A: Again, that might embarrass somebody.

J: Right. Better to let the opportunity slip by.

A: There is that turmoil inside. Wondering if we're even acknowledging during the day that we are concerned about the spiritual.

J: A Jesus freak.

A: It's been very difficult for me to accept the idea that Jesus would live for one minute in my soul. Yet I know he sends messages to me that come from the soul, and words come from my mouth reflecting thoughts from the soul that I didn't know were there.

J: That's really well put. There he is.

A: Yet if I try to connect with Jesus, like first thing when I get up in the morning and get on the internet, I'll swing around and face the sculpture of him to say good morning and within minutes my mind is wandering into what has to be done today.

J: But that's where you spread your spirituality. Today. Right here. Right now. On earth. With the people we meet each day.

A: I think what slows me down is the fact that I associate quiet time with the world of guilt-and-punishment that has been with me since childhood and has affected my entire life. A kind of fear underlies it.

J: That somehow Jesus is a symbol of the guilt-and-punishment?

A: Something like that. Yet I know he is with me all the time if I just remember to open the door, and I've seen him at work with the people I've been assigned to. I just kind of get out of the way, and he does the fixing.

J: Again, that's pretty well put. I'd say you're pretty well adjusted.

A: Adjusting, maybe. Then, there's that silent, lurking fear that if I get too close to the spiritual, I'm inviting more trial and sacrifice than I want.

J: Ah, that, too! I think that's universal. That's what keeps a lot of people on the periphery. But I've never heard it expressed like that. "If I get too close to the spiritual, I'm inviting more sacrifice."

A: Isn't that what Jesus stands for? Sacrifice?

J: Absolutely.

More Sexual Abuse

A: We talked before about sexual abuse within the clergy.

J: I remember. Believe me.

A: Today I'd like to point out that there shouldn't be too many people pointing fingers.

J: I like the sound of that. Where are you taking us?

A: That there's a sexual abuse taking place in most of today's marriages.

J: Whooee. That's a broad statement.

A: No pun intended.

J: No pun intended.

A: But yes, broads, as wives, are half the problem. Husbands are the other half.

J: You suggest that something ugly is taking place in most marriages.

A: No. Something beautiful is *not* taking place.

J: A vanishing act?

A: At least, diminishing. Look around. Everybody's getting fat. They're eating more of everything that isn't good for them, in the kitchen, to compensate for not getting any satisfaction in the bedroom.

J: Another silent agreement?

A: Exactly. They don't have to talk about it. Just share another double chocolate brownie mix from the supermarket.

J: With a scoop of ice cream.

A: Of course.

J: Guilty! But Mary and I had a healthy sex life. Diminishing, as you say, over time, but we never stopped trying.

A: Not many people can say that. In the Stephen ministry program, most of my assignments are marital problems, separation and divorce, and at the base of it is the lack of intimacy, the intimacy that was a basic source of the relationship in the first place.

J: Really? You feel that the root cause of a break-up is the lack of intimacy?

A: Yes. The man calls it sex. The woman, intimacy. Yes, follow the pattern. Like in the old movie, The Seven Year Itch. The young couple falls in love, gets married, the lust is well served, kids come along, the couple has less private time and more responsibilities, they're both working, they're buying things they can't afford, they start to look at each other getting fat, maybe it takes nine or ten years, but the Itch appears in the man's head, or crotch, and all hell breaks loose.

J: It's all his fault.

A: Well, today, a lot of wives are the ones getting fed up and taking off. I had three cases like that. The women were making good money, they were less dependent, they would get some attention from some guy who isn't getting attention and they make the move. Bingo. Blended families, or in most cases, unblended.

J: But you contend that at the base of it is a lack of intimacy.

A: Absolutely. Our lifestyle today is consumerism. Just keep buying things, and eating things, that satisfy our daily needs, pills included, and we won't have to bother with that sex thing. Messy. The husband buys into it, figuring that will please her and maybe she will find time eventually to jump into bed and not roll over right away.

J: Wrong.

A: Wrong, is right. Sex, the lack of it, the lack of intimacy, is a root cause. It's closely related to the lack of talking about it. We don't talk about it, because that might lead to doing something about it. Like having a date night, or at least a date time once a week, or every other week, but agreeing on a time and place to make sure that it is an absolutely essential part of their lives together.

J: Instead of a hit and miss and awkward experience when it might happen.

A: You get it.

J: You're right, and that really underlines the point we've made before, that if couples do not talk about sex, that makes it easier to not talk about anything personal, anything that might embarrass or make the other feel uncomfortable. It's easier to avoid an argument, just soak it up and keep it inside.

A: We do it ourselves, and we know that our wives are doing it. And it all builds up inside. Then out comes the series of little put-downs, the I'm right and you're wrong nasty retorts, the explosions, the hurt, the silence.

J: The silence. That's the killer. Maybe for days.

A: And it drives a deeper wedge into any chance for intimacy in the relationship.

J: When will we learn?

Counseling counts

A: When you and Mary were counseling together, were you meeting mostly with couples, or where were your clients coming from?

J: We backed into it, very honestly. People we knew started coming to us in an informal way, and we kind of looked at each other one day and said maybe we should hang out a shingle, as the saying goes.

A: Start charging people you *didn't* know.

J: Right. It was all word of mouth.

A: You're good at that.

J: Among the other people. You know what I mean. We started with friends, and they would tell others about us.

A: You two offered an unusual combination of theology and wedded bliss.

J: Not exactly wedded bliss, but yes, we had unique backgrounds to offer. Cloistered in the first half of our lives, and suddenly knee deep in the problems married people face.

A: Did people often ask if you two knew each other back when you were cloistered?

J: All the time. We laugh about it now, but at the time, we were always surprised.

A: People like to think that maybe you two had been fooling around while you were in uniform.

J: That just *maybe* we were tempted like everybody else. No way.

A: Did you fall back on the scriptures much when you were counseling married couples?

J: No. Not really. Once in a while, a gem would emerge from my archive.

A: I believe that.

J: Actually, Mary ended up doing most of the counseling of couples. She had a Masters Degree in Counseling, and she was good. a good listener, and she could get right to the problem areas. People loved her, because she was so kind in the doing.

A: What were you doing?

J: I was still on assignment to the Prisons and teaching at NC State. I would sit in on Mary's sessions and help develop some approaches.

A: Were they mostly marital?

J: All kinds of problems. At the same time, we were having problems of our own. We had brought my Mother down from Connecticut and found a nice apartment for her, but it became apparent that she needed to be in a nursing home. All that going on while we were trying to make a living.

A: But I'm curious about the counseling, where your clients came from, how they heard about you.

J: Friends, mostly, like I say. We never made a formal announcement or placed an ad, but we did get written up in a newspaper column. We were both counseling inmates about to be released, Mary at the Women's Prison. I guess people figured if we could do that, we could do anything. I was also giving talks to various groups.

A: Were people accepting the fact that a former priest and nun could counsel people in the trials of married life?

J: Yes. In fact, I think they thought they were getting a bonus from the spiritual arena, and don't forget, I heard a lot of stories in the Confessional. I had a pretty good idea about the trials of family life as well as married life.

A: Give me an example.

J: We worked with one couple who were ready to get a divorce. He had lost is job, a good one, and couldn't find his way into another one, and he was bitter. His wife had gone back to work and was doing well. Their kids were in middle school and high school, and they were used to a pretty high standard of living and not too happy with making adjustments.

A: Typical situation today.

J: We were able to get him back to the Lord. I say back, but there wasn't a strong link to begin with. He started working on an assignment basis and eventually joined a couple of other men in a successful startup. Not the kind of money the family was used to, but enough to restore his self worth, and even the kids came around.

A: And the wife?

J: She stuck it out. Once he got back on his feet, their respect for one another was revived. They began to realize that they could live on less, which they did. Sold the big house, down-sized, and the kids learned a valuable lesson.

A: Happy ending. Or *beginning.*

J: We did some freebies, too. Young boy next door. Had built a following mowing lawns, ours included, and we got talking one day. Very shy, had a Single Mom, two younger sisters. I sensed that he might have a problem with porn, and I was right. Had been on the computer during the night.

A: Ouch.

J: I got him to get on his knees instead.

A: How?

J: Simply by opening him up to the opportunities he had, if only he'd get them in perspective and start working toward them, instead of filling his mind with low-life.

A: He needed a father figure. You, of all people.

J: You laugh.

A: I'm smiling, I'm not laughing. I think it's wonderful. Did he come around?

J: Beautifully. Instead of looking inward all the time and feeling inferior and compensating all that with porn, he opened up to people. His Mom had no idea of what happened, what he went through, but she was proud of the way he changed.

A: Another wonderful story.

J: We had a lot of them. Broken homes, divorces, illness, unemployment was a big one.

A: Did you find that a lack of communication was common to the broken marriages?

J: Very much so.

A: That's what we found in Stephen ministry. You and I have touched on it before, but man and wife are reluctant to talk about, to really exchange their honest feelings about, anything that might be a little embarrassing. Like sex. Intimacy.

J: Yes, and over time, that makes it easier not to talk about anything else that might be important to their marriage.

A: You found that to be the case in your counseling, too?

J: Absolutely.

A: Strange, yet completely understandable. We don't want to bring up a subject that we know will end up in an argument. One that might affect the relationship for weeks or months.

J: Or forever.

A: Ironic, that in a second marriage, couples are ready to put the cards on the table.

J: They learned the hard way. Now, they're going to have an understanding.

A: Or there won't be a beginning.

J: Right.

A: We learn a lot in counseling others.

J: Right.

Paideia pronounced Piedayuh

A: Tell me some more about Paideia. I know it goes back to the Greeks.

J: That was Plato.

A: He was in the middle, right?

J: Of what?

A: It's always Socrates, Plato and Aristotle.

J: Right. Plato wrote *The Republic* which was all about a future society of perfection.

A: Like ours today.

J: Yeah, hardly. No, he was trying to lay out what was necessary to achieve some kind of perfection in the way we live our lives. In all society.

A: Like the ten commandments?

J: No, that's another story. Those came later. These guys were b.c. you know. No, Plato was laying out the kind of education that would be necessary in order to achieve some kind of perfection. He called it *paideia*.

A: Funny, he gave it a Greek name.

J: He was trying to get across that we have to educate in a process that features the physical and spiritual as well as the mental development. Education of the total individual. That's what *paideia* means.

A: Ah, now I get it.

J: You remember when we went over to Terry Roberts' office, over at UNC?

A: Yeah, but I only half understood what they were doing.

J: They are trying to get school systems to put it into the regular curriculum.

A: Including the spiritual?

J: Sure, you can study the spiritual, the religions and all, without taking sides.

A: Gotcha.

J: It's more a way of teaching. A lot of discussion, instead of all lecture and memorizing and tests.

A: Kids don't have to memorize anymore. It's all there in their hand-held.

J: Plato was incredible. He regarded the idea of democracy as a "charming form of government."

A: As in unrealistic?

J: He advocated that a leading philosopher should run the country.

A: Wouldn't that be a hoot. We'd have Mark Twain up there.

J: No, he makes too much sense.

A: "Never slap a man who's been chewing tobacco."

J: You sure have a way of bringing it home.

A: Intellectual.

J: Plato asked a lot of questions, like what is reality? What is knowledge? What makes a thing a thing? Knowledge, for example, he says knowledge of reality is individual. Would be different for you and me. Knowledge is not universal. It's personal.

A: I'm starting to get worried about you.

J: You like Plato. He points out that reality is always changing.

A: I think I understand that one.

J: But he thinks there is an unchanging higher reality of goodness or justice, an ultimate truth.

A: We could have some fun trying to draft a philosopher king to run the country.

J: Maybe Deepak Chopra?

A: No, he's too American. Maybe Mother Theresa if she were around.

Disciplined Disciples?

A: I was wondering about the Disciples.

J: What about?

A: Do you think any of them were gay?

J: Oh my. No, I don't think any were gay, but I don't have any facts to back up that suspicion. Can I ask, what made you think of that?

A: I don't know, but I just like the idea of being a Disciple, and it occurred to me that we don't know too much about the originals, other than the fact that they were rough and ready fishermen, at least three or four of them, and they weren't too bright. They weren't quick enough to recognize that Jesus might be a little different even when he took their last two fish and five loaves of bread and fed a million people.

J: The fish weren't biting that day. And it was 5,000.

A: We don't even know if they were married, or if they had any kids, not that wives or women in general were of any importance then, but I'm concerned about how they made a living or whether they were always drawing unemployment.

J: We don't know too much about them. A few writers have attempted it.

A: One Biblical scholar, James Efird, says that Paul and Barnabas disappeared together for 16 years. He didn't suggest anything beyond that, but I like to speculate. Paul was always going on about being a dreadful sinner and never feeling worthy. You'll grant me that.

J: Dear God. Where did I find this man?

A: Come on. You were a priest. You know that some priests interpreted celibacy as not fooling around with *women*. Jesus never left explicit instructions. Or implicit, either. So I was just wondering, that's all. I really don't care if they were all gay. They could have showered together for all I care.

J: They didn't shower in those days.

A: So the Lord charges them with the responsibility to go out and spread the word.

J: You're going to suggest that they didn't go?

A: Not right away. They weren't really convinced until the Lord appeared out of nowhere and reminded them that he died for them, to hammer home the point.

J: You've been reading the scriptures.

A: So now what's the *word*? Are we to believe that these rough fishermen are suddenly endowed with public speaking skills, more important, with the word?

J: Yes.

A: I believe that, too. Not because it makes any sense, but because some of us have experienced something similar happening in our own lives.

J: Like in your Stephen Ministry?

A: Yes. I've said a few prayers over people breathing their last breaths, and the words came from somewhere else. But the Disciples were on a world tour for the rest of their lives. They were making big speeches to big crowds. Which raises another question. Only Jesus could make himself heard to a crowd of, say, 5000.

J: I don't know. Probably a digital sound system.

A: But what I really want to know is what did they preach? What was the word?

J: What is this, a quiz? We assume they talked about Jesus, the son of God. The God on earth.

A: That's what I want to hear. Not the Old Testament? Not Moses and the Ten Commandments? Not Noah and his Ark? Jonah in the Whale?

J: I'm sure they got a lot of questions about those in the Q&As that followed the slide show. Remember, that's what they were used to hearing. The Pharisees were the only real teachers before Jesus came along.

A: OK. I'm happy. We don't really know how many went on tour and why they waited so long to get going. Maybe they were like us, full of good intentions.

J: They must have been pretty convincing. Think of all the Cathedrals people have built ever since.

A: I'll bet they featured fear.

W h o   s a i d   t h a t ?

A: That quote of Cicero's has stayed with me.

J: He nailed it, didn't he?

A: How did they get so smart back in ancient times?

J: They even had plumbing.

A: There are lots of countries who still don't have plumbing.

J: Or water to flush with.

A: Don't you wonder what the world will be like in another 2000 years?

J: I don't think we'll be around.

A: We're told that people in Roman times, Jesus' time, figured the end of the world was just around the corner, the next generation would get the axe.

J: That's the general consensus, yet man has built cathedrals and monuments of all kinds ever since, in every generation, so they must have believed that there would be more generations to come.

A: Pyramids, Temples, Shrines. So how do we know that man won't still be around in the year 4005?

J: What would be our legacy? The century between nineteen twenty and two thousand twenty?

A: Wars, man! World wars, two big ones! And several smaller ones where almost as many people got killed.

J: I was thinking more along the lines of the automobile, telephone, television, the internet, you know, progress of sorts.

A: Yes, but. I think man will go right on hailing the wars. Look how we mark history by the wars of the time, Revolutionary War, Civil War, World War One and Two, the Korean War, Vietnam War, and those were just our wars.

J: I was about to say that we don't really memorialize wars, but we surely do. I think about all the statues in the Parks, with Generals on horseback.

A: We don't see any computers captured in clay.

J: One of man's great contributions was the atomic bomb which obliterated two Japanese cities.

A: We've been winning the arms race ever since.

J: Not a pleasant legacy. Fortunately, we can find some balance in the advancements in the computer world, the incredible progress we have made on the internet and now the social network and the I-pods and pads, and the speed of those advancements.

A: Cicero just turned over in his grave. He'd probably say, "You call that advancement? You haven't moved an inch toward peace."

J: We've had that conversation. Let's get back to quotations.

A: OK. Here's one I like: "Remember, people will judge you by your actions. You may have a heart of gold, but so does a hard-boiled egg."

J: I like that. Who said it?

A: Famous guy named Anon.

J: Anon also said, "People don't care how much you know until they know how much you care," but a lot of people have taken credit for that one. I like to think it was Norman Vincent Peale.

A: The one you quoted the other day was Lao-Tzu. "He who knows things is learned. He who knows himself is wise."

J: Here's another one I used a lot, "Pay deep, loving attention to a flower, a dog, or a person, and each will open up to you."

A: I love that one. That's beautiful. I don't think I've ever said anything profound.

J: "There are two ways to spread happiness. Either be the light that shines or the mirror that reflects it." That's Edith Wharton.

A: "Some people grumble because roses have thorns. I rejoice because thorns have roses." A. Karr said that. I wonder what the A stands for.

J: Arugala, maybe. We could go on all night quoting people.

A: Great reminders on how to live our lives.

J: Jonathan Swift said, "May you live all the days of your life."

A: How many of us do that?

Affection deficit disorder

A: You mentioned before that your parents weren't very affectionate.

J: True.

A: Not with each other, and not with you.

J: True.

A: Mine weren't either. In fact, they were talking in grunts a lot of the time.

J: Maybe it was the times. The great Depression and all that. I never saw my parents kiss.

A: I can't remember seeing that, either.

J: I think it goes deeper than the times. It's a personal thing.

A: Yes. Maybe a natural pattern in married life.

J: Well, a pattern, anyway. I think you're referring to the cycle of friends: lovers, mates, parents, empty nest, and then, *what happened?*

A: They've grown apart in the process. You married late with no kids. Did your affection fade away?

J: No, honestly. Not really. Oh, maybe Mary wasn't as demonstrative, but I still slobber all over her.

A: I've noticed. Maybe the fact that you didn't grow apart in raising a family has something to do with it.

J: A lot, I think. That's the part of the pattern we missed.

A: In most of the marriages I've witnessed, the bickering over situations or even minor decisions starts with the kids. The respect husbands and wives have for each other gets lost in disagreements, most times petty disagreements, but by the time that the kids strike out on their own, that collection of disagreements is monumental, and now the parents have more time to level put-downs at each other.

J: We've touched on this before. The affection has been directed to the kids, and the partners are left wanting.

A: Absolutely. I think we see the cycle start all over when the kids get married and start their families.

J: So affection between most men and women occurs before marriage and during the first years together. And sometimes when a couple reaches their twilight years.

A: Yes. Like us. We suddenly realize our days are numbered and we better, quick, start righting some wrongs.

J: Do you think it's possible for men to show affection for one another?

A: Well, not in public, probably, but certainly in private, at least we can *feel* affectionate toward one another without putting our arms around someone or patting him on the butt. I think of Army life where you're living in close quarters and sharing some difficult times, you gain a lot of respect for one another, a lot of trust. There we are again with Nouwen's two elements of a good relationship. I felt a lot of that with my two buddies, Slats and Foley.

J: We had similar conditions in the Jesuit life, and I'm still in touch with several of my old friends.

A: When you were in the Jesuits, and Mary was a nun, and you worked on projects together, I'm sure you felt a real affection toward her, toward each other.

J: Absolutely.

A: Did it ever go beyond that, like, "Gee, I wish I weren't in uniform"?

J: Did I ever have the thought? Of course. But you learn to dismiss those thoughts, that becomes second nature.

A: You were already married to your Maker.

J: The vows came first. Simple as that.

A: I'm really more interested here in family affection, or the lack thereof. Men, in general, are regarded as incapable of showing real affection. As the traditional provider and head of the house, they are not expected to show compassion or any tenderness. That's a woman's role.

J: Right. But it wasn't always that way. Right up until the mid eighteen hundreds, women worked right alongside men in the fields and men were real partners in raising the kids and doing the dishes.

A: The Industrial Revolution changed all that.

J: Right. That's when the corporate giants first got together and said, "Hey, we don't want women to get in on the spoils, start running companies and all that. We have to keep them home taking care of the kids."

A: The Cult of True Womanhood. I remember reading about that.

J: That's exactly what they did. Mounted a campaign putting the woman on a pedestal, the symbol of moral virtue, the righteous leader of home and family.

A: So history tells us that's where it all started. Affection was replaced by doing things for one another. The husband provides the financial support, the wife takes care of the house and raising the kids. Kind of an unfair agreement in the first place.

J: That was all changed with World War Two when so many women entered the workforce, but the traditional premise exists today – that the woman, the wife and mother, still bears the top responsibility for raising the kids, and taking care of the house.

A: The husband still finds time to play golf.

J: The computer, technology in general, has done a lot to level the playing field. Women expect a lot more sharing of responsibilities in today's marriages.

A: Well, they may be disappointed. Man is reluctant to give up his independence, even today when so many are unemployed, no longer the ultimate providers. Most of them find it difficult to become Mister Moms fixing the meals and running the kids to soccer practice.

J: The affection has disappeared in the maze of new, and drastic, changes in their roles.

A: The man has tough time swallowing his pride, and he's not at home being at home.

J: Tough enough if they're both working and trying to share the family responsibilities, maybe with a nanny or part-time help.

A: The workplace today, all the part-time, flex schedules, and contract assignments instead of a steady job, all that contributes to frazzled relationships for husbands and wives.

J: It's a shame, because a little affection goes a long way.

A: Amen. That's what's missing. A little hug, a kind word. A nice look.

J: We're too busy. We're all taken up with busyness.

A: We've lost track of what's important.

J: Excuse me for a minute. I'm going to give Mary a hug.

Fat Abstinence

A: Ever notice how many fat people there are walking around?

J: Yes.

A: I dropped my wife off at the supermarket. She was just going in to get a couple of things, so I waited for her in the car. I was kind of watching people go in and out.

J: You started counting fat people?

A: Right. Six out of ten were overweight. Three out of ten were actually obese.

J: Some of the kids, too, I bet.

A: I didn't count them, but yes, that's a good point. Fat parents have fat kids.

J: So, what are you going to do about it?

A: Well, I'm going to cut back on the fattening stuff myself. We have a lot of crackers and cheese and peanuts when we have that glass of wine.

J: It's so easy to over eat.

A: My point, I guess, is that it isn't healthy for Americans to be so fat. Fortunately, you and I have only an insignificant sign of a pot belly, so we can talk about it.

J: I like that description.

A: I think what's behind it, of course there are a lot of reasons, a lot of influences, but I think a case could be made that compensation is a root cause.

J: Not workmen's compensation?

A: Funny. No, but them, too. I think we compensate for the lack of something in our lives by eating things that taste good.

J: Ah-ha. You're appealing to my psychoanalytic leanings.

A: Enter the fray.

J: Well, you make a point, but I'm interested in the root cause theory.

A: Lack of sex.

J: Oh, I should have known.

A: People compensate because of a lack of sex. They eat. That causes a lot of problems.

J: I see a national campaign looming in the mind of my marketing-oriented friend.

A: There's a chronic need for one, but it will never happen.

A: No? Why?

A: Because the gods of advertising are spending billions a day to get us to eat their junk food. A few of the green people may get a column on the internet once in a while, or a magazine may get some brownie points with an article they know won't influence anybody for more than a moment.

J: A little guilt thrown in with the glitter?

A: Right. I think we're doomed to be a fat nation. The coming generations are going to see a lot more diabetes, a ton of people, pardon the pun, in hospitals having operations and suffering the consequences.

J: Did you read where mistakes in hospitals are the third leading cause of deaths?

A: Yes, either missed diagnoses or serving up the wrong meds or a dozen other possibilities.

J: But I think you're on to something with the root cause theory. Let's get back to that.

A: You can almost spot it among your friends, even church groups, maybe especially church groups. You see it in the way couples relate to one another. Or don't relate. And some don't hesitate to put down their partners in front of others. It's like a payback, "I'll get back at you here for putting me down at home."

J: Yes, I've witnessed that. We all have.

A: Men are getting back at their wives for lack of sex. Sex has been put on the back burner. Maybe the wife is working, or maybe just frazzled with taking care of the kids, and she's taken up with the busy-ness of our times, the speeding up of life with the cell phones and texting and the pressures of everyday life and the avalanche of advertising and never having enough money to cover the expenses.

J: It all adds up to lack of sex?

A: Right. One of the unwritten agreements that results is sharing involvement in a different activity: eating. It's a lot easier, they can do it anytime, they can shop together and make decisions together on the kind of ice cream and cakes, you know, that the kids will like, and they easily forgive each other for getting fat. Maybe there's a hidden plus, that if the partner gets some extra girth around the middle and the butt, he or she will be less attractive to someone else.

J: The roving eye will settle elsewhere.

A: We all have a roving eye. Most of us can undress a woman with only a quick look.

J: You express things so delicately.

A: Well, think about it. The root cause applies across the entire spectrum. Whether a couple is doing very well financially or if the husband is out of work. Maybe especially if he's out of work, because his self-worth is at a low point.

J: He gets the feeling that he doesn't deserve the extra attention in bed?

A: They don't talk about it. Maybe she is providing the major source of income and is automatically calling the shots.

J: He may be fixing dinners and doing the shopping.

A: Mister Mom. Role-reversal. Now she determines the if and when.

J: Meanwhile, they're eating well.

A: Yes, gobbling up the wrong foods.

J: They're compensating.

A: Right. They're compensating day in and day out, maybe at McDonalds with all the French fries, or the extra doughnut with the Dunkin Donuts coffee, that's my nemesis, or maybe she is stopping on the way home from work and bringing an entire box of doughnuts.

J: Instilling some bad habits for the kids. Meanwhile, you're saying that he keeps thinking about the great figure she had when they first married.

A: Right. If he's still working, maybe that roving eye is settling on one of the secretaries there.

J: If he's not getting it at home, maybe there's an opportunity at work.

A: That's what I'm saying. The lack of sex is the root cause of marital unrest.

J: We could say that the couple's lack of talking about it may be the root cause.

A: Yes. That's the kinder way of saying it.

Editor's note

Jack died in April of 2010, three days before his 90th birthday, the result of an auto accident and a broken neck. He was on his way to his favorite Gypsy Divers pool where he swam laps. He made a wrong turn, then a quick U-turn into the path of an oncoming car.

Several of us paid tribute to him at the worship service. Here's what Alan said:

Hope is the thing with feathers that perches on the soul and sings the tune without the words and never stops at all. That was one of Jack's favorite quotes. Another, was one about friends: *a single soul in two dwellings.* Sometimes Jack would get carried away with quotes from Aristotle and those other old dudes, and I'd have to slip one in from Mark Twain, like *Never slap a man chewing tobacco.*

If Jack were here, he'd be laughing along with us.

Jack was fun.

I'd pick him up, load him in the car, and off we'd go to the K&W Cafeteria. He loved the fact that I have a *Mustang* and people would see him getting out of a hot car. Go inside, there's these lanes of people inching their way to the food lane, all kind of glum, eyes on the floor, not really looking at each other, and Jack would immediately say something to the guy next to him and the people in the next lane and they'd be laughing and people in the other lanes would join in, and in minutes the whole place would come alive. He'd get to the food lane, kidding with the ladies behind the counter and he'd be calling them by their first names and they'd be serving up double portions to him. Finally get to the cashier and he'd get in her face, singing, *"Oh, Spanish Eyes."* Then the waitresses would be competing to see which one would get to carry his tray to the table, and as he makes his way, leaning more heavily on his cane, of course, because now there are people watching, he spots a pretty little girl and turns to the woman seated next to her, and asks "Is this your daughter?" and she says "No, I'm her *grand*mother." We couldn't guess, white hair, a sea of wrinkles. If he spotted a little boy, he'd say, "You know, they say when you look at the face of a child like this, you see the face of Jesus." It could be a Jewish family at the table, or Hindus, but it wouldn't matter.

When we'd get back to their condo, which Norm found for them so that they could live independently again, we'd start talking about some heavy duty stuff like the meaning of life, our purpose in life, end of life, life hereafter. Jack loved Woody Allen's line, *I don't believe in the afterlife, but I'm taking a change of underwear just in case.*

Jack and I came from two totally different walks of life. He was *born* into priesthood, a Jesuit for 30 years. I was raised Catholic, but I was always a little confused, and for 20 of Jack's 30 years in the priesthood I was apart from God. I felt that he had rejected me, so I was going to get along without him. Foolish me. Yet when Jack and I talked about the meaning of life or our purpose in life, we were often on the same page.

With all that training, a PhD in Psychology as well as Theology, he never once made me feel inferior or questioned my faith. He loved my background. He loved the fact that I had done all these crazy things in my life, like driving a taxi in NYC. He *envied* me for that.

We even wrote a few prayers, just for fun. Here's a short one, our favorite, *"Lord, help me do what you would have me be."*

Mark Twain also said, *"Never miss a chance to shut up."* So I'll close now with some conjecture we gave to the afterlife. We didn't buy that our souls would be wafting up through endless space to some distant Heaven where St Peter would present us with a harp and assign us to row 10,684. No, we thought the Lord God Almighty who gave us life, on earth, would have something else in mind, like maybe our souls staying close by, just out of reach, but joining the millions of souls who have preceded us, circling the earth, *just out of reach,* so that when they spot a like soul down here in trouble, a broken marriage, serious illness, kids on drugs, mom in a nursing home, whatever, they can immediately send down the strength, patience, courage enabling that soul on earth to get through that trial, and keep the faith. Our souls become the messengers of God's grace. The Divine Providence!

Would that be so bad?

I feel that Jack's soul is right there, connected to your soul and mine for the rest of our lives.

Printed in the United States
By Bookmasters